EDUCATION OF THE HEARING IMPAIRED CHILD

Edited by
Frank Powell, MA
Terese Finitzo-Hieber, PhD
Sandy Friel-Patti, PhD
Donald Henderson, PhD, Director

Callier Center for Communication Disorders
The University of Texas at Dallas

Taylor & Francis Ltd
London

COLLEGE-HILL PRESS, San Diego, California

Published by
Taylor & Francis Ltd, 4 John Street, London WC1N 2ET

First published by College-Hill Press, San Diego, California
Copyright © 1985 by College-Hill Press, Inc.

British Library Cataloguing in Publication Data

Education of the hearing impaired child.   130790
    1. Deaf—Education
    I. Powell, Frank
    371.91'2   HV2430   150.52
✓ISBN 0-85066-503-5   Pow

This edition not for sale in the American continent.

Library of Congress Cataloging in Publication Data
Main entry under title:

Education of the hearing impaired child.

    (The Callier monograph series on communicative
disorders)
    Bibliography: p.
    Includes index.
    1. Hearing impaired children–Addresses, essays,
lectures. 2. Deaf–Education–Addresses, essays,
lectures. 3 Deafness–Addresses, essays, lectures.
I. Powell, Frank. II. Series.
HV2437.E38   1984   371.91'2   84-22994
ISBN 0-933014-36-8

Printed in The United States of America

EDUCATION
OF THE
HEARING
IMPAIRED CHILD

The Callier Monograph Series
on Communicative Disorders

Series Editor
Donald Henderson, Ph.D.

CONTRIBUTORS

Ursula Bellugi, EdD
The Salk Institute for
Biological Studies
San Diego, California 92138

Sandy Friel-Patti, PhD
Callier Center for
Communication Disorders
University of Texas at Dallas,
Dallas, Texas 75235

Ann E. Geers, PhD
Central Institute for the Deaf
St. Louis, Missouri 63110

Edward S. Klima, PhD
University of California,
San Diego, and
The Salk Institute for
Biological Studies
San Diego, California 92138

Harry Levitt, PhD
Speech and Hearing
Department
Graduate School and University
Center
City University of New York,
New York 10036

Donald F. Moores, PhD
Center for Studies in Education
and Human Development
Gallaudet College
Washington, DC 20003

Kenneth L. Moses, PhD
Resource Networks, Inc.
Evanston, Illinois 60202

Ross J. Roeser, PhD
Callier Center for
Communication Disorders
University of Texas at Dallas
Dallas, Texas 75235

Hilde S. Schlesinger, MD
University of California,
San Francisco
San Francisco, California 94143

CONTENTS

Chapter 7.   **Evaluating Changes in the Communication Skills of Deaf Children Using Vibrotactile Stimulation**
Sandy Friel-Patti and Ross J. Roeser

INTRODUCTION

The Callier Monographs in Communication Disorders are based on the Bruton Lectures held at the Callier Center for Communication Disorders. Each series of Bruton Lectures and the resultant monographs focus on a central issue of human communication and its disorders. The individual volumes are designed not to be a comprehensive presentation of an issue but rather to be a set of provocative points of view by distinguished contributors.

The first Callier Monograph is devoted to the Education of the Hearing Impaired Child. This is a particularly appropriate topic because no other area of communication disorders is so plagued by controversy and, conversely, so poor in data to resolve these controversies. In the first chapter, Dr. Moores provides interesting insights into the slow pace of developing knowledge in education of the deaf and then continues with a thoughtful review of the problems and primary trends in education of the deaf.

The next section focuses on scholastic matters. Drs. Bellugi and Klima, in the last ten years, have provided new insights into the cognitive structure of American Sign Language (ASL). Dr. Geers takes a different tack and explores the educational limits of deaf children when all factors contributing to academic performance have been optimized.

The third section deals with personality and familial factors that complicate the process of educating a deaf child. Dr. Schlesinger develops the interesting hypothesis that the delayed linguistic competency of deaf children stems from parallel maladaptive coping strategies of other disadvantaged populations. Dr. Moses describes the grieving process that parents of deaf children go through and how resolution of this grieving process ultimately affects the deaf child's relations with its most important teachers—the parents.

In the final section, the discussion turns to technological advances that may play important roles in education of the deaf. Dr. Leavitt explores the potential impact of computers and computer aid instruction on education of the deaf. Drs. Friel-Patti and Roeser describe the potential additional educational benefits from complementary information delivered through a vibrotactile aid.

Section I

INTRODUCTION

Chapter 1

Educational Programs and Services for Hearing Impaired Children: Issues and Options

Donald F. Moores

In general, the progress of ideas through educational research has been slow, particularly in the fields of education for the deaf. Over the past several years there has been interest in the relationship between theory and practice, that is, the application of knowledge. It is clear that much research is trivial or irrelevant, having been conducted by researchers unaware of the real needs in the classroom. Conversely, because of the lack of communication between researchers and practitioners, the results and potential benefit of much excellent research has never reached the classroom.

It is difficult to have a clear perspective on the trends in educational programming and research because of linguistic factors. Because research in education of the deaf is often interdisciplinary, individuals from different disciplines often use the same terms in different ways. In order to minimize the possibility of misunderstanding, the following terms are defined:

Program Research. Program research refers to the relating of many discrete research activities to a common well-defined goal or problem area within the context of a single theme. This program provides the investigator with the flexibility to shift gears, to follow up new leads or drop approaches found to be nonproductive. A programmatic research activity is generally used to address a broad, particular question with a multifaceted approach.

Research Projects. These represent discrete individual projects which are designed to answer specific research questions. Such research does not ordinarily require the multifaceted resources necessary for research programs.

Demonstration Projects. The demonstration project is designed to translate into operation research results, sound observations and new ideas. This type of project provides the opportunity to bridge the gap between what is known and what can be done.

The foregoing definitions have several implications. First, very little programmatic educational research has ever been conducted. Several years ago, a review of a document by the Contract Research Corporation (1976) showed that the bulk of the research involved discrete projects of short duration spread across a large number of universities. Little or no evidence of educational benefit from this diverse shotgun approach was found.

The situation was worse in the area of deafness than in any other category. Not only was there little program research, there was relatively little project research. It was found that deafness was the only area to which government funding provided more support for *demonstration* activities than for *research* activities. Much of what has passed for "research" on deafness bypassed the research phases and was designed to demonstrate the effectiveness of methods or techniques to which the investigators were emotionally committed.

In a series of reviews on the application of child development research to exceptional children, Gallagher (1975) constantly reiterated the tremendous difficulty inherent in attempting to master several fields. Given the complexities of the problem, it is unrealistic to expect investigators to have competence in more than one discipline. Therefore, systematic progress usually does not come about as the result of discrete projects. For true progress in addressing complex problems, the concept of "idea dominance," that is, a clear, explicated, recognizable idea that should serve as the focus for work (Petrie, 1976), might be used.

In discussing patterns of federally supported research, Mueller (1968) made the following statement:

> In the past, support related to the education of the handicapped was largely limited to individual project grants.
>
> Those were, generally speaking, of relatively short duration and were designed to answer fairly specific research questions. The present trend is toward support of research programs, although not to the exclusion of support for specific projects. This pattern is more efficient, allows for better integration, provides for program continuity, and institutionalizes major research efforts . . . . Integration of individual programs bearing on a given problem which may cut across various areas of disabilities and various research disciplines is another advantage of this pattern of funding. From the point of view of the researchers, is the continuity provided by program support is a particular advantage. Support is for a longer period and lapses of funding are avoided. (p. 52)

RESEARCH AND DEMONSTRATION

Demonstration activities may be seen as part of the process of applying new knowledge—the results of research—into action at the instructional level. Gallagher, the first Associate Commissioner of the Bureau of Education for the Handicapped, described the practice of providing financial support to individual researchers as a "very simplified 'knowledge into action' model" and characterized the results as "a magnificent failure" (1968, p. 485).

Perhaps the most common mistake has been the tendency to invest in demonstration activities which have no theoretical basis and which are not based on objective data. In discussing educational research around the world with the handicapped, McKenna (1974) concluded that the amounts dispersed for development and delivery of educational services were far more substantial than the investment in research. There is a tendency to support demonstration activities that are not knowledge based in the area of hearing impairment. Hurder (1974, p. 194) has claimed that service oriented concerns exceed knowledge oriented interests in our field.

Such unsystematic support for non–knowledge based demonstration projects, which typically provide subjective self-evaluation, not only detracts from research activities but also can be detrimental to children by fostering inadequate and poorly documented practices and inhibiting the development of alternate procedures. The poorest example of this unsystematic support was the original series of early intervention demonstration projects for the hearing impaired, which were funded across the United States from Massachusetts and New York to California. Although the projects had some beneficial components, such as parent involvement, most were locked into rigid, constrictive patterns of communication that essentially ignored academic and cognitive considerations. There was no evidence of awareness of research trends and findings in areas such as psycholinguistics, child development, cognition, general education or even education of the hearing impaired. In the few cases compared with early intervention programs that did not receive federal funding, results in the non–knowledge based demonstration projects were relatively poor. As federally funded demonstration projects, however, such activities are perceived as bearing the federal government seal of approval even if they are neither knowledge based nor even reasonably effective. The situation will not improve until the acquisition of knowledge is a prerequisite for application.

THE ACQUISITION OF KNOWLEDGE AND THE APPLICATION OF KNOWLEDGE

There is more than one way of categorizing the continuum of research to application, but it would be well to bear in mind a distinction between the research process—the acquisition of knowledge—and the application of knowledge (Garner, 1971). The interrelationships of research and application must be carefully defined; isolation of one from the other is destructive. It must be emphasized that interaction is mutually beneficial to both theory and practice.   '

For education in general in the United States, as well as for special education, a gulf has existed between representatives of scientific (research) and service (educational) disciplines. McKenna (1973) notes

> In the past, a great deal of educational and psychological research has been done in academic isolation as a partial requirement for a degree or by scholars in their spare time from teaching, with or without funds. Such projects derived from an individual's interest in a special problem or from the availability of subjects for research. As a result, little work was done on broad issues with practical implications requiring investigations for protracted periods of time by members of different professions. This often had the effect of reinforcing inertia and insuring a kind of built-in conservatism with regard to innovation in educational establishments. (p. 24)

The process by which the discovery of new knowledge is accomplished and eventually translated into educational innovation is a complex one which may be viewed as extending over a series of identifiable stages. Gallagher presents five phases (research, development, demonstration, dissemination, and adoption) into an ongoing educational operation (Table 1-1). Each phase requires a different emphasis, concentration of professional skills, and organizational support.

The ultimate criterion of successful applied research is the initiation of changes in the service delivery systems that are of demonstrable benefit to children. Anything less than beneficial change should be unacceptable. A major component of any research must be careful consideration of the means by which results can be used to ameliorate the condition of hearing impaired individuals.

The present time lag in American education between the initiation of research activities and adoption of changes can be attributed to a number of factors. A basic obstacle is presented by the fact that the research and the adoption ends of the continuum have been previewed as the separate domains of colleges and public schools, respectively, two types of organizations that currently address themselves to different orders of priorities. At the college level the priorities and reinforcements have been arranged in such a way as to encourage behavior that tends

Table 1–1. Phases of Translation of Knowledge to Action

Developmental Phase	Purpose	Supporting Organizations
Research	The discovery of new knowledge about handicapped children or about those intellectual and personality processes that can be applied to these children	Usually research centers and institutions, often found in universities, which can provide organizational support for long range attacks on difficult research problems
Development	Knowledge, to be educationally useful, must be organized or packaged into sequences of activities or curricula that fit the needs of particular groups of children	Sometimes done through research and development centers which concentrate on sequencing of existing knowledge; basic setting is still the university
Demonstration	There must be an effective conjunction of organized knowledge and child; this conjunction must be demonstrated in a school setting to be believable	A combination of university or government and school cooperation required; usually, the elementary or secondary school is the physical setting and additional resources are supplied by the other agency
Implementation	Local school systems with local needs usually wish to try out, on a pilot basis, the effective demonstrations they have observed elsewhere to establish its viability in a local setting	Additional funds for retraining personnel for and establishing a new program locally are needed; some type of university, state, or federal support is often needed as the catalyst to bring about this additional stage
Adoption	To establish the new program as part of the educational operation; without acceptance of the policy level, demonstration and implementation operations can atrophy	Organized attempts need to be made to involve policy decision makers (i.e., school board members, superintendents) in the developmental stages so far; items like cost effectiveness need to be developed to help make decisions

From Gallagher, J.J. (1968) Organization and special education. *Exceptional Children*, *34*, 485–491. Reprinted with permission.

to concentrate on research activities to the exclusion of other stages. Systems which rely exclusively on project by project funding reinforce this behavior. The outcome has been a closed system in which research is conducted frequently for the benefit of other researchers. In this way an individual might conceive of a problem, develop a design, run an experiment, and then report the results in esoteric jargon incomprehensible to the practitioner.

Researchers can succeed in their goal of influencing useful change only when effective communication is established with practitioners. The present system has produced two inevitable outcomes: (1) much research has been conducted that is clearly irrelevant to the needs of deaf individuals; and (2) much clearly relevant research has been conducted but has not been of benefit because of the lack of mechanisms for translating knowledge into behavior. Figure 1–1 illustrates the situation that results when the interaction between researchers and practitioners is nonexistent and when the translation of knowledge into action is blocked by misunderstanding and lack of cooperation between the two systems.

It is clear that the breakdown occurs at the point at which college-school cooperation should be at the maximum level, that is, at the *demonstration* stage, which, in Gallagher's terms, involves an effective conjunction of organized knowledge and child. For any such conjunction to be believable it must be accomplished in a real-life setting. Without an effective bridge, there is little confluence of knowledge and practice.

For the schools to progress, they must be open to inputs from a number of sources, with the colleges providing a significant impetus for innovation. If researchers are to exert a major influence they must to a greater degree adopt a learner's role and be more sensitive to the needs of children and to the realities of the home, workplace, and classroom. For an idea to be accepted it must stand the test of empirical verification in the field.

Ideally, both the schools and colleges should function as partners in all phases of the continuum from research to adoption. Although the colleges should assume the major responsibility for the first stages, the schools must be able to influence the type of research activities undertaken. Later, the colleges should contribute their unique skills to the evaluation and modification of programs that have been adopted into the ongoing educational operation. Figure 1–2 presents an ideal university-school symbiotic relationship.

Much of the work of the Center for Studies in Education and Human Development at Gallaudet College presently involves school-based activities. It is apparent that the problems faced are different from those

Figure 1-1. Traditional perceived disjunction of the missions of universities and schools. From Moores, D.F. (1973, December). Moving research across the continuum. In J.E. Turnure Ed. *American Psychological Association Symposium Papers.* University of Minnesota Research, Development and Demonstration Center in Education of Handicapped Children. Occasional Paper #24, p. 51.

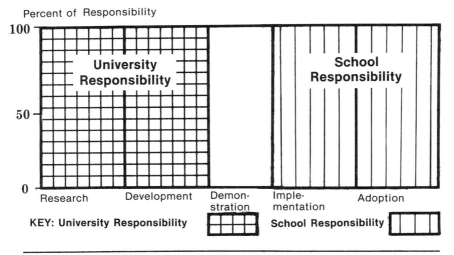

encountered in more tightly controlled research-based activities. Although the problems may not be any more difficult, at first glance, they certainly appear to be. This may be explained in large part by the fact that most researchers have been trained to design, conduct, and report research within a tightly controlled, highly constrained framework. The reward systems of most universities serve to keep a majority of investigators within this model.

The move into the classroom usually represents both a relative loss of control and the introduction of numbers of potentially confounding variables. We continually have to acquire new skills to meet the changing demands of conducting relevant applied research.

Not only should the social and bureaucratic skills that involve dealing with the groups of children, teachers, principals, and assorted administrators be considered, although this type of expertise is essential, but in addition issues such as sampling techniques, assessment of change, instrumentation, formative and summative evaluation, and development of behaviorally defined objective should also be kept in mind. If growing numbers of scientists are allowed to bring their talents to bear on these areas, new relationships will develop between researchers and practitioners, which will prove to be of greater benefit to deaf individuals than the present system.

Figure 1–2. Ideal university–school sharing of responsibility. From Moores, D.F. (1973, December). Moving research across the continuum. In J.E. Turnure (Ed.), *American Psychological Association Symposium Papers*. University of Minnesota Research, Development and Demonstration Center for Education of Handicapped Children. Occasional paper #24, p. 51.

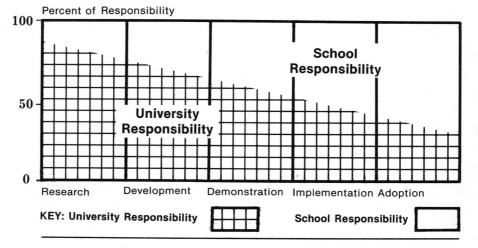

THE PRESENT AND THE RECENT PAST

There is little doubt that the field has undergone enormous changes in the past 10 to 20 years. Most of these changes have been beneficial. Many of the forces behind the changes—both general and specific— can be identified quite readily. Clearly, we have been influenced by societal developments such as the Civil Rights movement and a greater acceptance of cultural pluralism. Moves toward deinstitutionalization and passage of legislation such as Section 504 and PL 94-142 reflect the spirit of the times.

We have also been influenced by demographic realities. For example, the post–World War II baby boom in the United States continued until around 1960, longer than in other industrialized countries. Since then the numbers of children born stabilized and then began to drop, with eventual effects on elementary and secondary school education with which we are so familiar.

In the area of deafness the impact and implications of the falling school-age population was masked by the rubella epidemic of the early 1960s, which had a more fundamental and far-reaching impact on the field than any other identifiable cause. As education in general was facing the prospect of declining enrollments, schools were frantically trying to meet the needs of unusually large groups of deaf children moving through the system. At each step of the way—as the children grew—services and programs were developed and expanded, beginning with parent counseling and moving through preschool, kindergarten, elementary, and secondary years. These children are finishing their secondary education and are now presenting the same challenges to post–secondary education programs that they have presented to other levels of the school system.

There seems to be little awareness of the magnitude of the effort or the extent of success in responding to the needs of these children and their families. As in so many fields, we tend to concentrate on problems and shortcomings. Still, the majority of deaf children in the United States born during the rubella epidemic are growing up to be responsible, independent, and capable adults who will contribute to the benefit of society. Professionals involved in serving the deaf can and should draw a great deal of satisfaction from this fact.

One little understood phenomenon in the manner in which the children in this age group have permanently altered the field. At each level, programs have expanded and adjusted to serve deaf children, and at each level the mold has been broken. There is no reason to go back to the types of programs in existence in the past. The influence of these children will be with us for generations. To a great extent the presence of this population has been largely responsible for the two most significant developments in the field in the past generation: the growth of total communication and the establishment of both day and residential placement options.

A contrast can be illustrated by a brief look at the field of communication for the deaf just prior to the rubella epidemic, that is, the situation 20 years ago. A very short list provides an idea of its extent: oral-only, residential, elementary–secondary, and paternalistic. Very briefly, all programs for the deaf, to the best of my knowledge, were oral-only, at least up to age 12 years. Aside from separate day schools in some large cities, public school programs for the deaf were few and far between. In general, education was limited to the school years of kindergarten through grade 12. Preschool programs tended to be private, usually offered through clinics. Except for Gallaudet College, which has approximately 300 deaf students, post–secondary educational opportunities were almost nonexistent. The extent of paternalism only 20 years ago is hard to believe. Deaf people, with the exception of a few individuals associated with federal government, had little influence over the program that supposedly were designed to serve them. There was not one deaf superintendent of a school for the deaf.

By policy most public schools did not hire deaf teachers or other deaf professionals. Of course, the blame could not completely be placed on the public schools. There were almost no deaf people who were eligible for state certification. For example, at Gallaudet College the teacher training program was limited to the graduate level, and deaf students were not allowed into graduate school before 1960. Before that time, there were no deaf graduate students, there were no credit courses available in sign language, and no one was allowed to use sign language during practicum experiences in the elementary school.

Clearly, then, great strides have been made. Publicly supported preschool programs are available in most states. Classroom communications options range from oral-only to total communication. Placement options range from self-contained to mainstreamed. The trend is toward a true commitment to the concept of an individualized educational program. Rather than wasting energy over abstract issues concerning some hypothetical best method or best placement, there is more attention to fitting the program to the child. Although there is a long way to go, deaf professionals are beginning to take their rightful places as teachers, counselors, psychologists, and administrators. There has been a virtual revolution in the availability of post–secondary school opportunities; in addition to Gallaudet, programs are in effect at the South West Collegiate Institute for the Deaf, National Technical Institute for the Deaf, and California State University at Northridge, and there are regional vocational technical programs in Louisiana, Minnesota, and the state of Washington. Much of the success of these programs can be attributed to the use of qualified interpreters. As a result of their success with college-age students, more and more interpreters are being used with junior and senior high school aged children.

The view of the present status, then, is influenced by whether the glass is thought to be half empty or half full. In spite of the unquestioned progress, too many students still go into the world unprepared to deal with its communication, social, and vocational demands. Unacceptably large numbers have inadequate oral communication skills, many have not acquired levels of basic literacy, and more than a few lack the preparation to function and compete in our technological society.

In a recent discussion, some researchers were trying to agree on identifying the factors that account for most of the variance in the achievement of deaf children. In other words, what conditions seemed to relate most closely to academic success? The conclusions were somewhat disquieting. The following four conditions were agreed upon:

1. The severity of the hearing loss.

2. The age of onset of the hearing loss.
3. The socioeconomic status of the family.
4. The hearing status of the parents.

Quite simply, the greater the hearing loss, the more difficulty the child has linguistically and academically. Children who lose their hearing after acquiring language and speech do better than those for whom hearing impairment was present at birth or acquired by the age of two years. Children whose parents are college educated and affluent do better than those whose parents are less well educated or do not fare as well financially. Finally, children with deaf parents do better than children with hearing parents. If a child happens to be profoundly deaf from birth, the chances for academic success are greatest if he or she is fortunate enough to have two college educated deaf parents.

All of this may be very interesting, but it does not provide much information on what should be done. The extent of hearing loss, age of onset, family socioeconomic status, and parental hearing status are beyond control. It is the responsibility of professionals in this area to deal with the children as they are. The question, is how is it possible to make a difference? What can be done better, or differently, or more consistently that will help the children meet their human potential?

ISSUES AND OPTIONS

At this point, some areas that deserve further consideration will be examined. In each case, some issues will be identified, options presented and discussed.

Several issues can be touched on. First, for example, the advisability of a thorough evaluation of methods of teaching reading to deaf children, with a possible complete restructuring of the present curricula, needs to be dealt with. Second, there is almost no information of a sociological nature on the adjustment of deaf adults or their social and vocational functioning in society. Third, despite the fact that children are supposed to receive an individualized educational program based on valid assessment instruments, there is a major lack of intellectual, linguistic, social, and achievement measures with norms for deaf children. Five areas to be considered are the following:

1. Parent-child communication.
2. Academic programs and special instruction.
3. Classroom communication.
4. The role of educational interpreters.
5. Secondary programs.

PARENT-CHILD COMMUNICATION

As increasing numbers of hearing parents have decided to add manual components to their oral communication interactions with their deaf children, the question has arisen over just what type of system to use. The consensus to date has been that hearing parents should first learn a relatively simple system rather than try to master all of the complexities of the language used by deaf adults known as American Sign Language or ASL. Stokoe (1975) presents this position as follows:

> [T]he sensible approach . . . described in the Williams' account can be followed by many parents and teachers if they will take the trouble to learn, not the whole vocabulary and system of a natural sign language like ASL, but a small vocabulary and simple grammar suitable for communicating with very young children. (p. 420)

Most of the systems used by parents are what is known as manual codes in English; that is, they follow standard English word order, frequently use initialized signs, and have invented signs for function words and bound morphemes such as *-s* (plural), *-ed*, *-ly*, *-ing*, and so forth.

By following English word order, these systems can be used in coordination with speech, and parents are urged to develop their skills in simultaneous oral-manual communication, Meadow (1981), for example, has stated that parents should be encouraged to communicate with children in ways in which they are comfortable. She suggests that for most parents this would entail the use of bimodal oral-manual communication.

The evidence that has accumulated indicates that parents can learn these manual codes with English and that the consistent use of such systems is positively related to the communication skills and academic achievement of the children. There is evidence also, however, that fathers usually do not develop adequate levels of proficiency in manual communications. How this failure can be remedied is not known, but it is one that must be faced.

Perhaps practical suggestions will present themselves or even a type of communication guide for hearing parents of deaf children will be developed from what is known of the process of language acquisition in hearing children combined with results of recent studies behavior of deaf parents with their infants.

For example, the basic elements of baby talk have been established across an impressive number of languages and even have been alluded to in writings of classical times. The term "baby talk" used here refers not to the ways babies talk but instead to the manner in which adults communicate with babies. Regardless of the language used, adults modify their communication systems in dealing with infants. There are changes in tone of voice, grammar is simplified, vocabulary is reduced, redundancy is higher, nouns are used more frequently and pronouns less frequently, affection is expressed regularly, and pet words are used.

A key question is whether parents can be helped to acquire skills in an additional modality without detracting from the warmth, richness, and spontaneity of the usual parent-child interaction behavior. It is not enough merely to master the vocabulary and grammar of a system. Those elements by themselves are artificial. Of more concern is human beings and how they behave. Function is more important than form.

Many linguists have concentrated on demonstrating that manual systems of communication can be fully developed linguistic systems, and their efforts have met with great success. To a certain degree there has been an interest primarily in the structure of ASL and efforts to demonstrate how it differs from spoken language. Much of the work has dealt with ASL in isolation without taking into account broader issues of communication and socialization.

The scope of work must be broadened to include similarities as well as differences and to look at more general issues of communication. The evidence is accumulating that deaf parents use a broad range of linguistic systems and modes of communication with their children, and the amount of speech used by deaf parents with their infants has been greatly underestimated. Maestas y Moores (1980) has identified 11 different modes of communication used by deaf parents with children during the first six months of life. They include speech alone, signs plus speech, fingerspelling alone, sign alone, signing on the child's body, and manually guiding the child through signs. An interesting finding is that speech alone and speech plus signs seems to be used more often with infants than sign alone. This casts doubt on the assumption of many people that ASL is the native language of children of deaf parents and that they do not learn English until later in life. The reality appears to be a great deal more complex and not enough information is available at present to arrive at general conclusions. There is optimism, however, that in the next five to ten years parents will be provided with more practical and useful help in establishing effective communication with their children.

ACADEMIC PROGRAMS AND SPECIAL INSTRUCTION

Acknowledgment of some fundamentally difficult issues and decisions about the nature of our programs may need to be made in the near future. These decisions will reflect where priorities are placed for the children served and the priorities that will need to be developed. Simply put, there are two major educational goals for deaf children. One is to reduce or eliminate the gap in academic achievement between deaf and hearing children in all areas, from arithmetic to history to science. The other is to develop the language and communication skills of the child to the greatest extent possible. Of course, these goals are not in conflict; children with better communication skills tend to achieve at higher levels. However, some questions may be raised. In a study of deaf children up to the age of eight years in educational programs in six states (Moores, in press), it was found that both speech and the use of residual hearing of children in two programs were superior not because of the modes of communication emphasized—one was total communication and one was oral-only—but because of the unusual amount of time and effort devoted to training. Most programs for deaf children devote large blocks of time to the development of speech, hearing, and English grammar skill. Even at the college level, the Gallaudet Prep Program and the National Technical Institute for the Deaf (NTID) Vestibule program provide intensive work on English skills.

The dilemma faced is in deciding where the time should come from to concentrate on these academic areas. The previously mentioned study (Maestas y Moores, 1980) also clearly indicated that deaf children lagged behind hearing children in arithmetic skills by six years of age. They also spend less time in arithmetic instruction than hearing children. Research on hearing children indicates that, all other things being equal, achievement in a particular subject depends on the amount of time spent on that subject. Unless the school day for deaf children is made one third to one half longer than for hearing children, the issue must be confronted openly. In a way, a decision was made generations ago without being articulated. The decision was to give academic achievement lower priority. Thus, even today, in any program for the deaf every class, regardless of content, is considered a speech class or an English grammar class. It may be best to continue in this vein, but the issues and consideration of possible effects of the various options should be opened for discussion.

CLASSROOM COMMUNICATION

In the past ten years or so, classroom communication for the deaf has changed from predominantly oral-only to predominantly combined oral-manual. The pedagogical systems employed have been manual codes with English, such as Seeing Essential English (SEE1), or Signing Exact English (SEE2), or Signed English. Although the results suggested that these systems are an improvement over oral-only instruction, criticisms have been raised over the theoretical background and practical implementation of each. One issue today that has major ramifications for classroom communication and for teacher training is the fact that the systems are based on morphemes, not on words. As a result the sentence "I walked to the shopping center" would have six spoken words:

I + WALKED + TO + THE + SHOPPING + CENTER

but eight signs:

I + WALK + -ED + TO + THE + SHOP + -ING + CENTER.

This has the effect of slowing down communication, although it is still understandable and may give more linguistic information. What we must find out is, first, if the slower rate influences information transmission and, second, if the additional morphemes really do help improve English skills. Kluwin (1981) found that hearing teachers increased their proficiency by incorporating elements of three dimensional space into their signing to increase the efficiency of the systems they used. It would be a mistake to develop yet another sign system—there are too many already. However, modifications in existing systems may be considered. There is one major problem. Kluwin found that the typical hearing teacher needed three to four years to develop good manual communication skills. Think of this in the context of the finding by Corbett and Jensema (1981) that the typical teacher of the deaf is only on the job for three or four years. In other words, by the time an average teacher has acquired good manual communication skills, he or she may be ending a teaching career in the field of deafness. If this is actually the case, the problems to be addressed are how to develop manual communication skills more effectively during training and how to encourage more people to make a lifetime commitment to this field.

THE ROLE OF EDUCATIONAL INTERPRETERS

With the impetus of federal support, programs for training interpreters for the deaf have been established in all parts of the country. Standards for certification have been established, and interpreting has been accepted as a profession in a remarkably short period of time. The documented success of so many post–secondary school programs for the deaf may be attributed in part to the establishment of effective interpreter services.

Based largely on success in post–secondary school programs, increasing numbers of secondary school programs have been using interpreters in classroom settings, and there are reports of interpreters in preschool and elementary school settings. A recent legal case dealt with the request by deaf parents for a classroom interpreter for their daughter in an integrated elementary school class. In this case the child had highly developed oral and manual communication skills. There was no doubt that she could follow the signs of an adult. In reviewing the literature, however, no reference to research or programs serving deaf students below college age was found. There simply is no information on the role, if any, of interpreters in elementary and secondary schools. The impact could be greater with older students. Questions about interpreting for young children who may not be proficient in either oral communication or a manual system have not been addressed. Implications of the presence of another adult in a relatively unstructured class setting have not been considered, nor have issues of cost effectiveness. Clearly, attention will need to be focused on the most effective utilization of interpreters throughout the educational system.

SECONDARY PROGRAMS

An area that is in need of great attention is the transition period from elementary to secondary levels of education. As children move from elementary to secondary grades in the American educational system, the most obvious difference is that the student populations of the secondary schools tend to be much larger than those of elementary schools. The need to provide comprehensive services leads to larger concentrations of professional personnel and resources. The necessity for specialized training causes the general elementary class teacher to be replaced by secondary subject matter specialists. At this age level, deaf students also require a higher concentration of specialized services and personnel as they leave the elementary years (Moores, 1982).

The transition may be even more traumatic for deaf than for hearing children. First it may involve a physical move away from home to a residential school. Under the best of circumstances this places new pressures on the child and on the family. If the child does stay at home—

for example, in a large, multi-district secondary school program for the deaf—secondary school attendance might involve commuting to a different school district after enrollment in a neighborhood elementary school.

A second major factor relates to classroom communication system. In many cases the child might have to make the transition from an oral-only to a total communication environment. For example, reports from the Model Secondary School for the Deaf indicate that large numbers of students enter the school with neither a residential school experience nor a knowledge of any system of manual communication.

Because there is very little information on present programs, a five year study is being initiated to identify the characteristics of secondary school–aged deaf children and the programs that serve them for the purpose of facilitating the development of truly effective secondary school programs for a range of deaf students.

The objectives of the study are the following:

1. To identify and describe in detail the major educational options available to deaf students of secondary school age.

2. To describe in detail the characteristics, including family variables, of deaf students enrolled in the various types of programs.

3. To evaluate separately the effectiveness of each type of program in meeting the educational, vocational, and social needs of deaf children and their families.

4. To develop separate guidelines for the implementation of effective programs to meet the needs of secondary school-aged students in various settings.

SUMMARY

In closing, it should be emphasized that applied programmatic research can and should play a much more active role in the field of Deaf Education. Five areas will face major questions and options: (1) parent-child communication; (2) academic programs and special instruction; (3) classroom communication; (4) the role of educational interpreters, and (5) secondary programs.

In each of these areas significant progress has been made, but it is clear that there is still a long way to go. It is appropriate to finish by quoting a saying that might have originated in the hills of Tennessee:

We ain't what we wanta be,
and we ain't what we're gonna be;
but, thank the Lord,
at least we ain't what we wuz.

REFERENCES

Contract Research Corporation (1976). *Twelve years of research on education for the handicapped.* Belmont, MA: Author.

Corbett, E., and Jensema, C. (1981). *Teachers of the hearing impaired. Descriptive profiles.* Washington, DC: Gallaudet College Press.

Gallagher, J.J. (1968). Organization and special education, *Exceptional Children, 34,* 485–591.

Gallagher, J.J. (Ed.) (1975). *The application of child development research to exceptional children.* Reston, VA: Council for Exceptional Children.

Garner, W.R. (1971). The application of knowledge: A symbiotic relation. *American Psychologist, 27,* 941–946.

Hurder, W.P. (1974). The United States of America. In J. McKenna (Ed.), *The present situation and trends of research in the field of special education.* Paris: United Nations Educational Scientific and Cultural Organization, pp. 147–270.

Howe, H. (1976). Education research—the promise and the problem. *Educational Researcher, 5,* 510–514.

Kluwin, T. (1981). The grammaticality of manual representations of English in classrooms using manual communication. *American Annals of the Deaf, 126*(5), 510–514.

Maestas y Moores, J. (1981). Early linguistic environment. *Sign Language Studies, 28,* 1–13.

McKenna, J. (1973). Introduction. In J. McKenna (Ed.), *The present situation and trends of research in the field of special education.* Paris: United Nations Educational Scientific and Cultural Organization, 11–66.

Meadow, K. (1981). *Deafness and child development.* Berkeley: University of California Press.

Moores, D. (1974). Moving research across the continuum. Paper presented at the American Psychological Association Annual Convention, Montreal, September 1974.

Moores, D. (in press). Early intervention programs for hearing impaired children: A longitudinal assessment. In K. Nelson (Ed.), *Children's language* (Vol. 5). Hillsdale, NJ: Lawrence Erlbaum Associates.

Mueller, M.W. (1968). Trends in support of educational research for the handicapped. *Exceptional Children, 34,* 523–527.

Petrie, H.G. (1976). Do you see what I see: The epistemology of interdisciplinary inquiry. *Educational Researcher, 5, 9–14.*

Stokoe, W. (1975). The use of sign language in teaching English. *American Annals of the Deaf, 120*(4), 417–421.

Section II

ACADEMIC CONSIDERATIONS

The development of language in young deaf children is a major concern to all educators of the deaf. The long-standing controversy of oral versus manual speech polarized educators of the deaf and reduced the issues of language acquisition of deaf children to a single one of modality selection. Deaf children's delay in developing language skills has been a persistent problem, which has affected children learning in an aural-oral tradition as well as those in manual programs. Only in the past decade has basic research on the language acquisition strategies of deaf children been initiated. In Chapter 2 Bellugi and her colleagues at the Salk Institute have systematically demonstrated that American Sign Language (ASL) is in fact a complexly structured language with a highly articulated grammar. This enriched understanding of sign language has also led Bellugi to some discoveries about the acquisition of language by young deaf signers. In their chapter, Bellugi and Klima report on three of the first morphological systems to emerge and be mastered by deaf children and how these systems are incorporated into the children's syntactic organization and discourse. The evidence shows that deaf and hearing children follow a remarkably similar course of development despite the differences in language modality. The deaf child analyzes the components of the language presented to him or her in the same "linguistically driven" manner that the normal hearing child does.

Working from an educational rather than linguistic perspective, Geers in Chapter 3 reports data gathered during a large standardization study investigating the English language skills of children from both oral programs and total communication programs. The children's scores on *Grammatical Analysis of Elicited Language—Simple Sentence Level* (GAEL-S) are reported for both groups. The detailed comparisons of the grammatical categories produced by oral and manual productions of the children is essential information for all educators of deaf children. Geers and her co-workers were struck with the overwhelming finding that the majority of profoundly deaf children evaluated, regardless of communicative modality, clearly were not realizing their potential to develop facility with the English language. The chapter by Geers concludes with a presentation of the findings of a three year project designed to explore the effectiveness of teaching efforts with elementary school-aged deaf children. The researchers and educators working on the *Experimental Program in Instructional Concentration* (EPIC) were charged with designing an ideal program without limits of cost, staff, materials, and space. Final testing of both the control and experimental groups is now completed, and Geers presents the comparative analysis of the two groups over the full three years of the study.

Chapter 2

The Acquisition of Three Morphological Systems in American Sign Language*

Ursula Bellugi and Edward S. Klima

As little as ten years ago, when there was as yet no evidence of a highly structured morphology in signed languages, suggesting a title such as the one heading this chapter would have been impossible. The explosion of research on the structural properties of signed languages, however, has made it clear that these forms of gesturing have been forged into complex linguistic systems in the hands of deaf people across a few generations. It is interesting that this should be so, given that deaf people do not form a geographic community (although, of course, the schools for the deaf provide an opportunity for interchange), and given that the forms found in the language still bear such striking clues of their origins in the representation, by the hands, of shapes, objects, actions, and events. When we began our studies in 1970, we maintained a listing of all the available manuscripts and papers on sign language studies, since they were so scattered, so few in number, and tended to be buried in obscure publications. We find that today it is no longer possible to keep up with the books and dissertations that are blossoming forth from different parts of the country, let alone with the new studies of signed languages in different parts of the world. In this chapter we first examine briefly some of the ways in which signed and spoken languages are similar and some of the ways in which they differ. The new understanding of sign language grammar has led to some discoveries about the acquisition of language by young deaf signers.

*From *Papers and Reports on Child Language Development*. Stanford University, 1982, *21*, K1–35. Reprinted with permission.

Modality and Language

Current research shows that American Sign Language (ASL) has developed as a fully autonomous language, with complex organizational properties not derived from spoken languages, thus providing a new perspective on human languages and on the determinants of language organization (Baker and Cokely, 1980; Bellugi and Studdert-Kennedy, 1980; Klima and Bellugi, 1979; Lane and Grosjean, 1980; Siple, 1978; Wilbur, 1979). Like spoken languages, ASL exhibits formal structuring at the same two levels (the internal structure of the lexical units and the grammatical scaffolding underlying sentences); it also reveals similar kinds of organizational principles (constrained systems of features, rules based on underlying forms, recursive grammatical processes). Yet the form this grammatical structuring assumes in a visual-gestural language is apparently deeply rooted in the modality in which the language developed.

Despite the commonalities in principles of organization between signed and spoken languages, there are aspects of linguistic form in signed languages that stand out most strongly as resulting from the differences in modality. These differences are not necessitated by the change in modality but are at least seductively invited by it. A fundamental difference between ASL and spoken languages is the iconicity that pervades the language at all levels.

Characteristically, lexical items themselves tend to be globally iconic, their form resembling some aspect of what they denote. At the morphological and syntactic levels, also, there is often congruence between form and meaning. Spoken languages are not without such direct clues to meaning (reduplication processes and ideophones provide direct methods of reflecting meaning through form, for example). In sign language, however, such transparency is pervasive. ASL thus bears striking traces of its representational origins, but at the same time it is fully grammaticized. Another difference is in surface organization: signed languages display a marked preference for layered (as opposed to linear) organization. The inflectional and derivational devices of ASL, for example, make structured use of space and movement, nesting the basic sign stem in spatial patterns and complex dynamic contours of movement. In the lexical items, the morphological processes, the syntax, and the discourse structure of ASL, the multilayering of linguistic elements is a pervasive structural characteristic (Bellugi, 1980). Although ASL is the most thoroughly analyzed of the signed languages of the world to date, other signed languages that have been examined so far suggest that these characteristics—iconic roots, preference for layered organization, and the structured use of space in grammar—are general across primary signed languages.

One might have every reason to believe that such surface differences between signed and spoken languages might influence the course of language acquisition. If the mapping between meaning and form is more direct than in spoken language, this might allow the child a more direct route into the language at all levels. The change in transmission system (from the ear to the eye, from the vocal apparatus to the hands) might in itself be expected to influence the course of acquisition. For example, in signed language, unlike spoken language, the articulators are visible and manipulable. This provides an opportunity for certain mother-to-child interaction that is not available for spoken language. In this paper we examine the extent to which such surface differences affect the acquisition of sign language by deaf children of deaf parents. Before presenting some of the first findings of our acquisition studies, we briefly describe the structure of the language as it is reflected in its morphology.

Three-Dimensional Morphology

The signs of American Sign Language are related by virtue of a wide variety of inflectional and derivational processes. Different base lexical forms have families of associated forms, all interrelated by strictly formal patterning, based on modifications of the movement of the signs in space. Thus a single root form, for example that glossed as ASK or QUESTION,[1] has a wide variety of manifestations, as shown in Figures 2–1 and 2–2. These different forms mark grammatical categories, such as person, number, reciprocity, temporal aspect, and distributional aspect on the verb, as well as form the basis for noun-verb derivationally related pairs and a host of other derivationally related processes. What defines ASL as an autonomous language is that its specific morphological markings do not match those of English in any way. In fact the inflectional devices are far more differentiated than those of English. The variety of inflectional and derivational devices indicate that ASL is an inflective language, more like Hebrew, Latin, and certain African languages than like English or Chinese (Bellugi and Klima, 1979; Klima and Bellugi, 1979).

In the *kinds* of distinctions that are morphologically marked, ASL is like many spoken languages; in the *degree* to which morphological marking is a favored form of patterning in the language, ASL is again similar to some spoken languages. However, in the *form* by which its lexical items are systematically modified, ASL may have aspects that

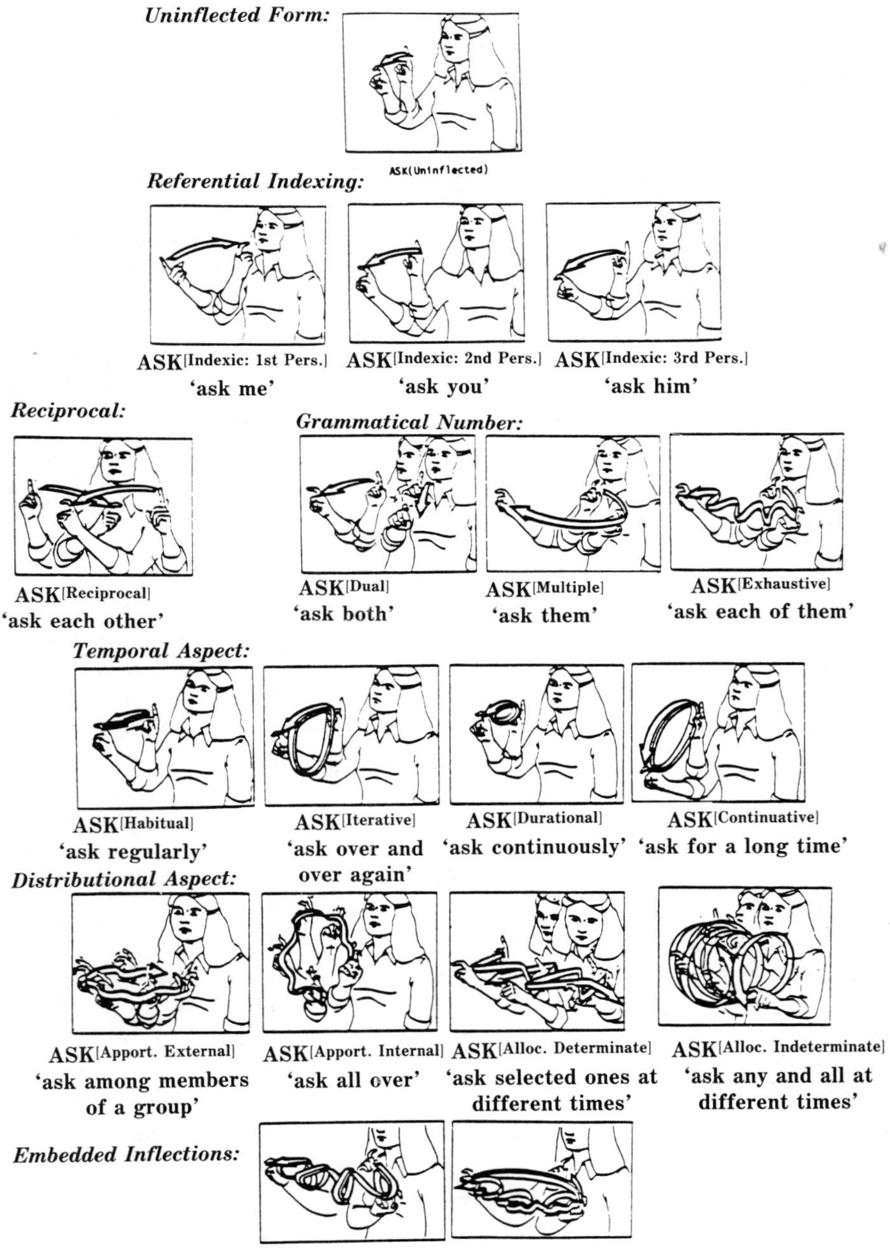

Uninflected Form:

ASK(Uninflected)

Referential Indexing:

ASK[Indexic: 1st Pers.]   ASK[Indexic: 2nd Pers.]   ASK[Indexic: 3rd Pers.]
'ask me'   'ask you'   'ask him'

Reciprocal: *Grammatical Number:*

ASK[Reciprocal]   ASK[Dual]   ASK[Multiple]   ASK[Exhaustive]
'ask each other'   'ask both'   'ask them'   'ask each of them'

Temporal Aspect:

ASK[Habitual]   ASK[Iterative]   ASK[Durational]   ASK[Continuative]
'ask regularly'   'ask over and   'ask continuously'   'ask for a long time'
                     over again'

Distributional Aspect:

ASK[Apport. External]   ASK[Apport. Internal]   ASK[Alloc. Determinate]   ASK[Alloc. Indeterminate]
'ask among members   'ask all over'   'ask selected ones at   'ask any and all at
of a group'   different times'   different times'

Embedded Inflections:

Figure 2-1. Inflectional operations on a single root: ASK.

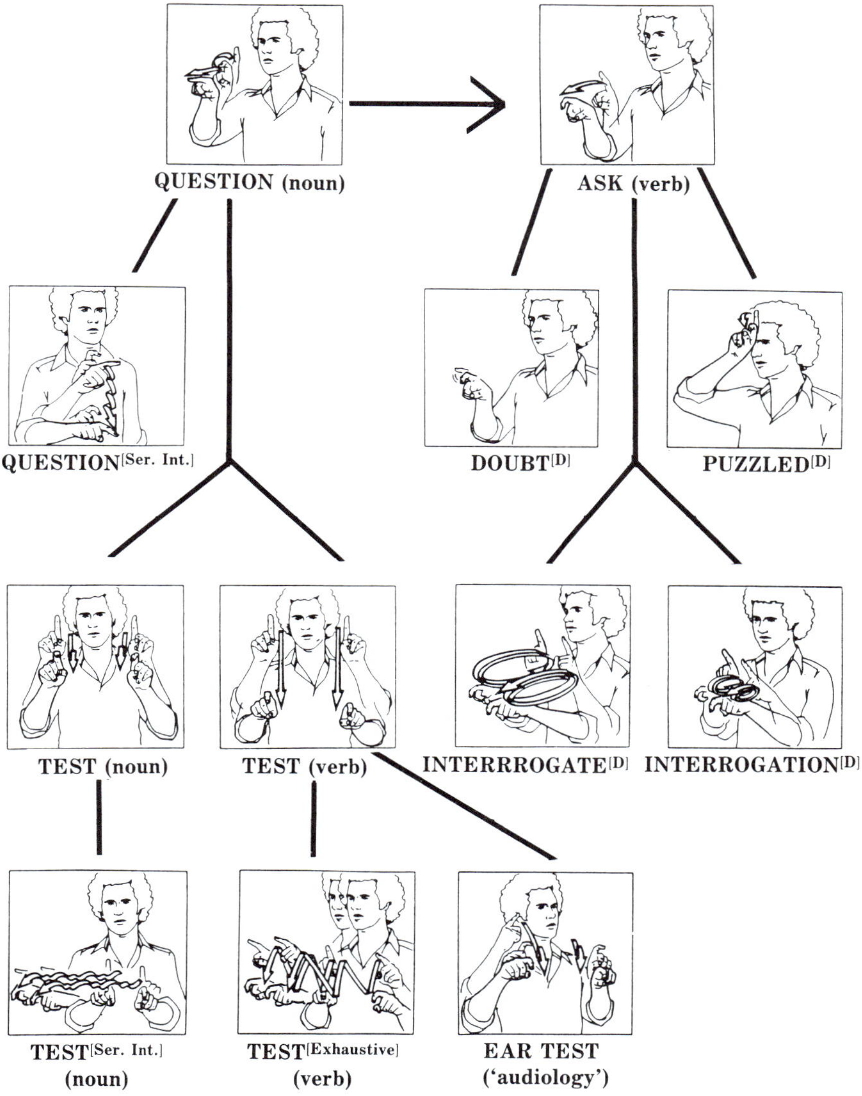

Figure 2-2. ASK/QUESTION and some related forms.

are unique. In a Semitic language such as Hebrew, words are composed of triconsonantal roots, with vowel patterning interwoven. These roots form the basis for a wide variety of distinct inflectional and derivational patterns. For example, k-t-v is considered to be the basis for such words as *katav*, 'write'; *ktiv*, 'spelling'; *katuv*, 'written'; *hitkatev*, 'correspond'; and so forth (Berman, 1978). It has been argued that these are appropriately analyzed as multitiered structures; the root as one skeleton tier, and inflectional and derivational morphemes each as a separate tier (McCarthy, 1979). But the final surface form of Hebrew lexical items no longer reflects its layered structure: *ktiv* differs from *katav* and *katuv* in the temporal arrangements of its sounds, represented as consonants and interleaved vowels. In ASL, which is similarly morphologically rich, families of sign forms are related via an underlying root: in the case of the forms in Figures 2–1 and 2–2, what is shared by all is a handshape /G/, a location (plane in front of body), and a local movement shape (closing of the index finger). Inflectional and derivational processes represent the interaction of this root with other features of movement in space (dynamics of movement, manner of movement, directions of movement, spatial array, doubling of the hands, reduplication, and the like) all layered, as it were, on the sign root. (Note that the morphological patterns themselves are often congruent with their meanings). This generates a wide variety of forms, such as 'ask you,' 'ask each other,' 'ask all over,' 'ask them,' 'ask each of them,' 'ask continuously,' 'ask regularly,' 'doubt,' 'test,' 'question,' 'interrogate,' 'interrogation,' 'inquire,' and many more. Unlike the examples from Hebrew, the surface forms of ASL inflectional and derivational patterns retain their tiered structure in the final output.[2] And yet the regularities that relate root and morphologically complex forms—the formal rules—are similar in the two types of languages.

We have chosen three subsystems that seemed to be the best candidates for showing modality effects in acquisition: the transition from gesture to symbol in pronominal signs; the spatial marking for verb agreement; and the formal distinction between nouns and related verbs.

THE ACQUISITION OF THREE SUBSYSTEMS

The Transition from Gesture to Sign

The system of person deixis in ASL gives rise to a particularly striking issue in the connection between transparency and grammatical system in the acquisition of language. Deixis in spoken languages is considered a verbal surrogate for pointing; in ASL, instead, it *is* pointing. The grammatical category of person is defined with respect to participant roles in discourse. First person is used by a speaker to refer to himself or herself; in ASL, the signer points to his or her own torso; second person refers to the addressee, and in ASL it is realized by pointing toward the torso of the person being addressed. These pronominal signs in ASL are, in fact, the same as the pointing gestures that hearing people sometimes use to supplement their words nonverbally. We may say, "I mean *you*" while pointing at a specific person to single him or her out. What is paralinguistic with respect to a spoken language, then, is a lexical item within the context of this fully developed gestural language. It is in fact part of of the indexical system involved with verb agreement. If these so-called pronouns are really just pointing, this should make the use, understanding, and acquisition of these forms very straightforward and cause them to appear early and error free in young deaf children of deaf parents.

The problems that young hearing children have with the acquisition of such terms as *I* and *you* in spoken languages like English are well known and have been documented. Such deictic terms all involve shifting reference, which is very different from names or nouns. Having agreed to call one person *Jane* or *Mother*, each speaker uses the same name. But with terms like *I* and *you*, the term does not apply to the person, but rather with a person's turn as speaker or as addressee. These "shifters," as Jakobson (1979) called them, present problems for young children learning spoken languages. Clark (1977) suggests that a child begins by using first person forms, and does so only sporadically at first, often in alternation with the child's own name; problems may arise when children begin to use the contrasting form, *you*. Clark posits that some children form the hypothesis that *I* used by an adult speaker is an alternative to themselves. Clark cites examples of such observations from a number of different studies and in a variety of languages. Several other studies recently have focused on this issue (Charney, 1980; Chiat, 1981, 1982; Deutsch and Pechmann, 1978). The child's "incorrect hypothesis" is generally corrected within a few months. By the age of 2;6 to 3;0 most hearing children have mastered such shifting pronominal terms.[3]

We had fully expected that the learning of the equivalent of pronominal reference in ASL would be easy and early ("trivial" is the way we expressed it). The hearing child's problems with the shifting nature of such arbitrary strings of sounds such as *you* and *me* are readily understandable; there is no clue in the form of the sounds to the referents. But in ASL, the pronoun signs are exactly the same as pointing gestures;

if I sign "YOU" and you sign "ME," we are both indicating (pointing to) the same person! With such obvious gestures, directness of reference would seem inescapable. When our early videotapes revealed that mothers tended to use names rather than pronoun signs with their children, and that the children did the same, and when parents told us that the children's misunderstandings of pronominal reference had motivated their switch to using name signs, we were very suprised. We had not, at that time, observed children unequivocally producing pronoun errors spontaneously. Frankly, we and other researchers could not imagine that deaf children would make mistakes in person reference by pointing. That is, not until we found the following exchange on one videotape of a deaf mother and her deaf child of 1;3 (Fig. 2–3A):

> Mother: WHERE MOTHER?
>   "Where's Mother?"
> Child: (ME)! (pointing to herself).
> Mother: (Mother looks surprised) NO!
>   (ME) MOTHER!
>   "NO! I'm mother."

The mother then took the child's hand, moved it so the child's arm was outstretched and made the child's hand point to the mother's chest, signing MOTHER with the other hand at the same time, for emphasis.

In our laboratory, Petitto has now taken on a serious investigation of the acquisition of pronominal reference in deaf signing children, combing through videotapes and setting up elicitation situations at critical ages (Petitto, 1983a, 1983b). It turns out, to our surprise, that for the signing child, this is not an error-free area at all; quite the contrary.

Petitto's involvement came about in a natural way. One day a deaf mother and her child (age 1;11) from our acquisition study came to visit the laboratory. We asked the mother (who had formerly been a researcher with us) whether the child ever made mistakes in pronominal reference. "No," signed the mother. "I don't think so." But at that point Petitto noticed the toddler pick up her own tiny red bathing suit she had chosen for herself, and then sign "SWIMSUIT (YOU)" (Fig. 2–3B).

The mother, a trifle embarrassed, signed, "NO, NO, NO. (YOU) MEAN YOU," making the pointing sign directly and forcibly on the child. This "correction" had no effect whatsoever; the child wandered around our laboratory blithely pointing incorrectly for reference to herself and others. In a language where the "speech organs" are directly visible and, moreover, manipulable, this kind of mother-child correction can take a remarkably different form than it does in spoken language. On several occasions, when the child reversed pronouns, the mother actually took the child's hand, turned it around, and moved it vigorously in the "correct" direction. To no avail. On the next opportunity the child persisted in making errors.

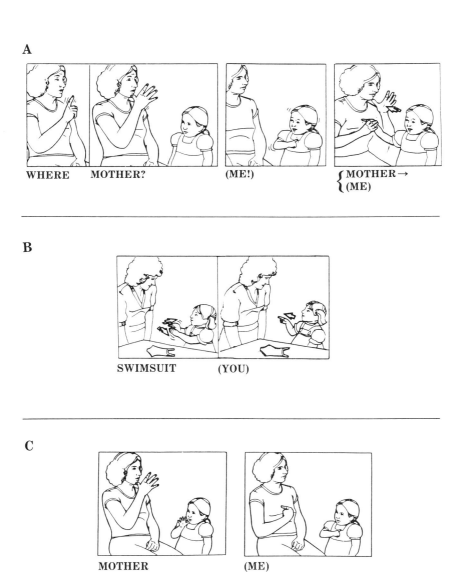

Figure 2-3. *A,B,* Child's incorrect pointing signs; *C,* child imitating signs.

What might lead the deaf child to overlook the simplicity of reference of the pointing gesture? One aspect may be that pointing signs in ASL share formal properties with other ASL signs: there is nothing in their form that singles them out as different. The sign glossed as "ME" is made with the index finger extended from a closed fist (hand configuration) with a contact (movement) on the torso (location). There are many ASL signs that share in just those properties: the same hand configuration occurs in the signs HOUR, CANDY, GO; the same location in FEEL, DRESS, ANIMAL; the same movement in FINE, VACATION, MOTHER. Thus, no aspect of their formational properties would indicate their special status as deictic pointing signs. Figure 2–3C, for example, shows a deaf child imitating the signs MOTHER and (ME). It might well be that the child in the early stages of acquiring signs assumes that the pointing sign (ME) is a formal name—perhaps an alternate name—just as is the sign MOTHER, and he or she might temporarily assume that they refer to the same person.

Petitto has now developed a series of tests for comprehension and production of pronouns for self and addressee, and she is collecting data across a series of young deaf children. What is striking in the data is that errors are evident in comprehension, and they are prevalent (as well as uncorrectable) in production. Petitto found in one deaf child the following distinct periods marking the transition from gesture to sign:

1. At ten months of age, the child pointed freely, using the extended index finger in a gesture that has essentially the same *form* as the ASL sign used for first and second person reference and for other pronominal reference. The child's pointing serves a variety of functions: for investigating, for indicating, and for pointing to herself and others.

2. During the following year (11 months to 1;9), something very dramatic happened in the child's use of pointing—one aspect of her pointing completely dropped out. While she continued pointing for investigating and for indicating objects, she no longer pointed to herself or to her addressee; apparently this was a transition stage. Hours of videotaped sessions during this period are completely devoid of this use of pointing that was richly represented earlier; however, the child did make reference to herself and others through lexical signs. During this same period, the child's language development was marked by a steady growth in the vocabulary of signs, stably used in a variety of contexts, and by the rise of multisign sentences.

3. Petitto found the first instance of a reemergence of pointing toward addressee when the child was 1;10. The child was hungry and apparently wanted something to eat. She signed "EAT, (YOU) WANT EAT." The mother responded in ASL, "No, I don't want to eat. I'll eat later." But

then the child went to get the basket with her food in it. The mother, realizing the child's error, signed the ASL equivalent of "Oh, you mean *you* want to eat." Thus, after one year's absence there appeared in an ASL sentence the first pointing sign directed toward the addressee, and it was a reversal: she pointed toward her mother to mean herself! The following month there was a surge in the occurrence of pointing signs for pronominal reference; and nearly all of them were incorrect. During this period the child appeared completely impervious to corrections by her mother—even to manipulative forms of correction, such as when the mother took the child's hand and twisted it around to point in the right direction. The consistency of these reversals and their resistance to correction lead Petitto to investigate the child's use of "I" and "YOU" in a systematic fashion.

4. Following the child over the course of the next few months, Petitto found that such pronoun reversals were resolved by age 2;3. The linguistic system by then matched that of the adult language. Petitto is now investigating this interesting phenomenon in other young deaf signing children.

Thus, there is dramatic evidence of the transition from gesture to sign. It is a transition marked by the emergence of a form used as a pointing gesture, its absence over a period of several months, and then the reemergence of the same form as a pronominal sign—now integrated into a linguistic system, but marked by systematic reversals. As part of a linguistic system the form appears to present to the signing child exactly the same problem as do arbitrary shifting terms across the world's spoken languages. It appears to make little difference, then, whether the pronominal terms are symbolized by arbitrary streams of sound segments as in spoken language, or by pointing signs, which are indistinguishable in form from pointing gestures. Deaf children, just as do hearing children, appear to have problems acquiring systems that mark shifting reference and require adopting shifting perspectives.

Deaf children learning ASL are not late in this kind of development. Their errors and their resolutions occur exactly on target with those observed in children learning spoken languages, neither early nor late. Thus, the directness of the relation in form between a pointing gesture and a pronominal sign does not prevent the child from taking certain garden paths on the way to the acquisition of the language—garden paths well attested to in the literature on the acquisition of spoken languages.

Whatever may be the correct interpretation of such reversed forms, their occurrence in these ASL learners suggests very strongly that the same strategies are being employed by deaf and by hearing children.

Language learning strategies prevail over whatever facilitative effects on the acquisition process may otherwise be inherent in the motivated nature of the linguistic form.

We have considered, so far, only one aspect of learning ASL, the pointing signs for first and second person as part of the pronominal system in ASL. We now turn to another subsystem that involves spatial loci: the level of inflectional morphology by which verb signs are systematically modified to indicate grammatical categories, such as agreement for person and number.

The Spatial Marking for Verb Agreement

Many spoken languages have verb agreement systems, whereby the form of the verb reflects certain grammatical categories of its arguments. For instance, in Latin, the verb varies in form (*amo, amas, amat*) depending upon person and number of its subject. In ASL there is also a system of verb agreement. Like the pronominal reference system in ASL, it is essentially spatialized: both utilize referential points in space as one of their morphological components. Verbs thus are not frozen, immutable forms, but undergo regular inflectional variation to mark person and number of their arguments. In function this system operates like verb agreement in spoken languages. However, in its form—marking connections between spatial points—verb agreement in ASL bears the imprint of the mode in which the language evolved. We first describe some aspects of verb agreement that have an iconic basis and thus might provide a different point of entry for the signing child; then we describe aspects of the adult agreement system and, finally, the steps by which the child masters the system.

The members of a large class of ASL verbs obligatorily "agree with" (or index) the locations of either one or two noun arguments. Such locations can be points in the signing space corresponding either to the location of the referent of an argument of a verb, or to an abstract location in space which the signer has established for the argument. Verb agreement in ASL has been described as pantomime in some earlier writings, and it is clear why it was so considered. When the addressee is the subject of the verb and the speaker is the object, the verb sign moves from a point corresponding to the location of the addressee to a point near the speaker; when the roles are reversed, the direction of movement is reversed. Thus the ASL sign equivalent of 'I give you' is the verb GIVE moving from speaker toward addressee (GIVE[X:1 to 2]). Since the image base of the sign GIVE is transferring an object by hand, this inflected sign form has much in common with the mimed act. For "you give me" the sign form moves from addressee to speaker (GIVE[X:2 to 1]). The iconicity of such an agreeing verb form is certainly direct, presenting a spatial analogue of the movement of the transferred object. The deaf child, on seeing mimetic forms such as the ASL equivalent of "I give you," "I give him," "you give me," might seize on this direct representation of sign forms to modulate the meanings of his or her signs; and the influence of such iconicity could very easily appear in the child's early signing.

Within the verb system in ASL there are several classes of verbs that behave differently with respect to agreement. Not all verbs mark agreement; of those that do, not all are marked in the same way. Among verbs that do not inflect for the loci of their arguments are SPELL, SAY, and LIKE. Some verbs have obligatory agreement (e.g., GIVE, TAKE, TELL); some optionally undergo agreement (SEE, SIT, BREAK); some can agree with only a single argument (WANT and SEE); some may agree with the spatial loci of two arguments (GIVE and LOOK-AT). Verbs also differ with respect to which argument is marked. However, the general mechanism for agreement on verbs is the same for all those that are indexable: movement between spatial loci established for noun arguments, in accordance with either loci for present referents or abstract loci associated with nominals in the discourse (Fischer and Gough, 1978; Klima and Bellugi, 1979; Padden, 1981, 1983).

How do children acquire a morphological system that is grammaticized, but which nevertheless displays a large amount of iconicity? Does the iconicity of ASL signs or grammatical processes give children a special way into language learning? Does iconicity have a pronounced facilitative effect on the mastery of the verb agreement system? Since the origins of such processes are so direct, the child might well begin via the mimetic basis of signs or inflectional processes.

Recently, Meier (1981, 1982), in our laboratory, has examined the role of iconicity in the acquisition of verb agreement. If the iconic properties of ASL signs are accessible to first language learners two and three years old, the iconicity of agreeing verbs should be highly accessible. The effects of such iconicity could be expected to appear in the acquisition of verb agreement. Meier developed three models that make specific predictions about what agreeing forms the children acquire early and what error types they produce. Two of the models make predictions based on iconicity: the first based on the relative similarities of agreement forms to mimed gestures; the second based on their relation to an analogical use of space with verbs of movement and transference. The third model makes predictions based on morphological complexity—a model that has been found to predict the course of the acquisition of inflectional systems in spoken language

(Aksu and Slobin, in press; Slobin, 1982). Meier's analysis of the acquisition of verb agreement in three deaf children of deaf parents[4] ranging in age from 1;6 to 3;9 (coupled with an experimental study of a group of such children) reveals that verb agreement is acquired by children within a narrow age range. In one child, for example, verb agreement begins at 2;0 and is complete by 3;0; at that point, the child is consistently providing correctly agreeing verbs across samples. We describe two periods in the children's acquisition of their first inflection:

1. Signing children around age two do not make use of the inflectional apparatus of ASL—including verb agreement—during the two and three sign stage. (The same phenomenon has been observed by Fischer [1973], Hoffmeister [1978], and Newport and Ashbrook [1977]). Even when young children imitate prodigiously, their imitations tend not to preserve featural markings of the morphologically complex forms of parental utterances. For conveying something as direct as "you give me," two year old children, instead of using the required agreeing form, sign the verb GIVE in its uninflected form, which resembles the mimed act of its opposite—"I give you!", and they sometimes add the separate pronoun sign, (ME). Children use uninflected forms in contexts in which the agreeing form is required with a variety of verbs (e.g., PUT, TELL, LOOK, SHOW, GIVE, LEAVE, TAKE). In one instance, the child signed GIVE[X:1 to 2] toward her mother, clearly intending "give me." The mother signed "NO" and pushed the child's hands back toward her in an effort to mold the correct form! Thus, the signing child first uses uninflected forms, even in contexts in which agreement clearly is required. The child does not enter the agreement system by exploiting the mimetic potential available within a visual–gestural language; he or she also fails to provide the grammatical markers required in the adult language.

2. Between the ages of two and three, the deaf children in our study began to produce various inflected forms of the verb (dual and aspectual inflections) but, first and most consistently, the forms showed verb agreement in contexts in which the referent is present. By around three, in series of deaf children, verb agreement is mastered in required contexts, and used consistently. The forms that children use and the errors they make en route to mastering the system support a morphological model of acquisition, rather than either an iconic model based on mimed actions or one based on an analogy with spatial displacement. For example, Meier (1981, 1982) finds that it is the morphologically more complex double agreement forms (even those that are more transparent mimetically) that are slower to be mastered.

We have observed a variety of overgeneralizations as the children begin producing inflected forms in earnest. Children provide agreeing

Figure 2-4. Children's overregularizations. *A*, Overregularizations of object marking on verbs; *B*, overregularizations of dual.

*SPELL[X: 'to me'] / SPELL   *SAY[X: 'to you'] / SAY   *LIKE[X: 'to it'] / LIKE

A Over-regularizations of Object-Marking on Verbs

*DUCK[N:dual] / DUCK   *BED[N:dual] / BED

*FUN[N:dual] / FUN

B Over-regularizations of Dual

forms for verbs that are not indexable in the adult language, such as SPELL, SAY, and LIKE, among others (Figure 2–4*A*). These forms are not mimetic or spatial analogic. The child inflects the verb SPELL for object (*SPELL[X:2 to 1]), meaning "spell to me"), although SPELL is not an agreeing verb. The child intending to sign "I say to you" inflects *SAY[X:1 to 2], which is not permitted in the adult language. The verb LIKE is overmarked for object—*LIKE[X:1 to 3i]—for the meaning "I like that." Furthermore, children extend verbs like DRINK and EAT to agree with the subject, when in fact these verbs are not indexable in the verb agreement system. Thus, deaf children, as they are working out the system for indexing verbs, overgeneralize to nonindexable verbs in a way that is quite analogous to English-speaking children's provision of *goed* and *holded* for past tense. These sorts of errors can be explained in the most straightforward way by a morphological model.

During this period, there are also errors in which the movement of the verb form is toward the wrong argument. For example, children inflect the verb GIVE toward the object to be given (e.g., *GIVE[X: "to plate"] HIM), for the intended meaning of "Give the plate to him," instead of toward the recipient (GIVE[X:"to him"]). These forms are both ungrammatical and counter-iconic; but they are, nonetheless, consistent with a morphological model; it is one of the grammatical arguments of the verb that is being marked but simply the wrong argument.

Thus, the weight of the evidence is entirely consistent with early morphological analysis on the part of the signing child and fits best with a morphological (not a mimetic or iconic) model of the acquisition process. The child does not make use of the iconic potential provided by the visual-spatial mode to enter the grammatical system. Rather, he or she begins with uninflected signs and then systematically analyzes the morphologically complex forms, as well as analyzing which verbs do and do not undergo agreement, what arguments are marked, and whether the markers are optional or obligatory. All of these aspects are worked out by signing children around the age of three; by then the ASL system for marking verb agreement is stabilized and mastered. In the acquisition of a grammatical subsystem of ASL in which one could expect a profound influence of iconicity, we find that iconicity has no facilitating effect.

The question, however, of the mapping between meaning and form in sign language and its role in the acquisition process is by no means fully resolved at this point. (See discussions by Brown, 1980; Launer, 1982; Meier, 1981, 1982; Newport and Supalla, 1980; Schwamm, 1980; and Slobin, 1980, for a range of views.) Other issues with respect to acquisition and transparency of morphological and syntactic forms remain to be addressed. We are now studying the acquisition of other inflectional processes across the series of children in our study. The next inflectional form to appear in children's signing after the marker for verb agreement is a dual inflection on verbs. In one of its forms, the dual is marked by a simultaneous doubling of the hands—certainly a direct and vivid expression of duality. This morphological marker, doubling of the hands, occurs in the grammar of ASL in a variety of inflectional forms other than in the dual inflection: *reciprocal* has the two hands directed toward each other; *characteristic aspect* is made with two hands in alternating circles: *distributional aspect* has two hands directed to alternating, nonseriated points. The semantic effect of these various forms that involve doubling of the hands ranges from 'to each other' to 'prone to' to 'action distributed across time'; there is no simple semantic common denominator (Klima and Bellugi, 1979).

As deaf children begin to provide the dual inflection in contexts that require it, they overgeneralize in interesting ways. For example, they do not limit the dual marker to verbs but sometimes overextend it to mark nouns and other categories as well, using two hands to indicate duality. They sign *DUCK[N:Dual] to indicate two ducks, or *BED[N:Dual] to indicate two beds, and even *FUN[N:Dual] to indicate "two people having fun" (Fig. 2–4B). These child errors are decidedly *not* options in the adult language; they are simply ungrammatical. One might consider that the child at this stage may be assigning some kind of transparent (admittedly iconic) semantic function (twoness) to a grammatical marker in the language (doubling of the hands) and overusing it for a brief period. We are pursuing these questions in further research.

The Formal Distinction Between Nouns and Verbs

Not only does ASL have a rich variety of inflectional markings, it also has a wide array of derivational processes, all of which are marked by movement distinctions in the language. There are derivational processes that form deverbal nouns (a form meaning "comparison" from the verb COMPARE); derivation of predicates from nouns (a form meaning "businesslike" and a different one meaning "proper" from the sign BUSINESS); nominalizations from verbs (a form meaning "the activity of measuring" from MEASURE); sentence adverbials from basic signs (a form meaning "instead" from DIGRESS); characteristic predicates from adjectives (a form meaning "vain" from PRETTY); and derivations for extended or figurative meaning (a form meaning "horny" from HUNGRY), and so forth.

Recognition of the derivational processes in ASL dates back only to about 1978 or so, when these processes were first described (Klima and Bellugi, 1979; Supalla and Newport, 1978).Before that time, analysts and signers alike thought that there were no principled ways to distinguish, say, a noun from a verb form, or nouns and verbs from any other form class. In fact, the groundbreaking *Dictionary of American Sign Language* (Stokoe, Casterline, and Croneberg, 1965) has signs listed according to their forms, and then specified for their use in the sentences. Thus there is a single sign form listed as a verb meaning "to sit," as well as a noun meaning "chair"; another sign form is listed as a verb meaning "to bicycle," as well as a noun meaning "bicycle," and so on for a vast number of signs. The implication was that, like the English word "drink," which is used both as a noun and as a verb, the same sign form in ASL is used in both nominal and predicate contexts. This was also the received view for many years of our own studies. However, starting late in life to become attuned to movement distinctions that might differentiate meanings in a visual-spatial language, we finally began to see a difference in the way a sign was made depending on its use as a noun or verb in a sentence. The first impression was that a noun form sometimes seemed "smaller" than the related verb form. Supalla, a native ASL signer who was then a researcher in our laboratory, investigated pairs of noun-verb signs (listed as single forms in the *Dictionary of American Sign Language*) and found systematic differences between them. His and Newport's important study formed the basis for a new understanding of the layer of grammatical processes in ASL, the kinds of movement feature distinctions required, and the kinds of rules that relate surface forms and abstract underlying roots (Supalla and Newport, 1978).

Thus, ASL signs (once thought to be single sign forms used in different contexts, much as words in an isolating language like Chinese are used without morphological markings for grammatical category) turn out to be split apart into whole paradigms of differentiated sign forms. The forms all share the same handshape, the same place of articulation, and the same movement shape (e.g., *circular, directional, wrist twist, nod,* and so forth) but are differentiated from one another by other features of movement: features such as *frequency, end manner, rate, tension, displacement,* and others (Klima and Bellugi, 1979). Verbs and their formationally related nouns are distinguished from one another in part by a manner differentiation: verbs end in hold or continuous manner; nouns have restrained manner of articulation. Thus there is a consistent differentiation in citation form between what is glossed as SIT-DOWN and CHAIR; RIDE-BICYCLE and BICYCLE; TELL-STORY and STORY; TO-TYPE and TYPEWRITER (Fig. 2–5A), and countless others. These forms would have separate listings in an expanded dictionary of ASL. Consider the pair BICYCLE and RIDE-BICYCLE in Figure 2–5A: /S/ hands circling repeatedly in alternation. The noun is differentiated from the verb only in that it has restrained manner (a signer can sense it in the articulation), and the resulting sign form is seen as smaller. That accounts for what we had noticed on our videotapes, as Supalla explained: the visible effect is smaller movement, but the motivating feature is an articulatory one—a slight tensing of the muscles. These featural differences mark pairs of forms throughout the language and are freely extended to nonce

Figure 2-5. *A*, Derivationally related noun-verb pairs in ASL. *B*, ASL noun, AIRPLANE, in normal signing, enlarged "stage" signing, and the "motherese" form, which is neither a verb nor a noun.

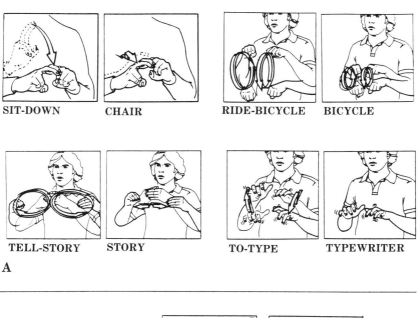

SIT-DOWN CHAIR RIDE-BICYCLE BICYCLE

TELL-STORY STORY TO-TYPE TYPEWRITER

A

AIRPLANE (noun) AIRPLANE ('stage' signing) *AIRPLANE ('Motherese')

B

signs and recently invented signs. Thus, the morphological marker distinguishing nouns from verbs is used productively in the language. The marking is subtle, at least to the eye of some non-native signers, but to eyes that have become more finely tuned to the movement features that mark morphological distinctions in ASL, it is evident that the formal markers differentiating nouns and verbs were there all along.

The prototypical cases of such noun–verb distinctions in the language are concrete nouns and associated action verbs. Not surprisingly, many of these have an iconic basis: many verbs in these pairs have an image base of action of the hands on or with an object (e.g., TO-TYPE and TYPEWRITER). However, such distinctions in the language are not restricted to concrete nouns and associated activity verbs (e.g., DERIVE-DERIVATION; MODULATE-MODULATION; SEARCH-EXAMINATION; GET-ACQUISITION; ANALYZE-ANALYSIS); and the image basis for a pair is often obscured. Still, the directness of representation might influence the course of acquisition. In terms of the form of the morphological markers themselves, it could be argued that the verb markers are motivated and the noun markers are not. There is some relation between aspectual meaning and formal marking for verbs: in general, single movement in the verb signs corresponds to single, punctual, or perfective action. Repeated movements in verbs refer to durative or iterative activity, made of repeated punctual actions (see Supalla and Newport, 1978, for further discussion). The noun marker is always repeated, restrained, and small; not an obvious formal marker for static objects! Furthermore, the noun marker often diminishes the iconicity of the image base, in that the sign movement no longer resembles the action. (We have noted that in general, grammatical processes in the adult language operate without reference to any iconic properties of the signs themselves [Klima and Bellugi, 1979, Chapter 1].) Thus, the verb OPEN-BOOK has an image base of hands opening a book (single movement). The noun sign BOOK has a restrained repeated movement that seems quite unrelated to what one would do with a book, thus obscuring its image base.

In 1982, only four years after the first description of the distinction between nouns and verbs, Launer, in our laboratory, completed a thesis on the acquisition of the derivational process in deaf children of deaf parents (Launer, 1982). Launer has amassed a formidable array of data on the acquisition of these morphological distinctions in ASL, from free signing on videotapes to a series of elicitation tasks, which she developed and first tested with deaf adults. She took seriously the description provided by Supalla and Newport, developed a feature system for encoding the morphological distinctions (e.g., *restrained, small, repeated*, for nouns, etc.), and noted the form of every noun and verb pair—including detailed descriptions of manner, size, repetition, and other features—in the signing of deaf children and their deaf mothers through several years. Using the data produced by the elicitation task (studying 32 deaf children of deaf parents across an age span of 2;0 to 11;0) and her analysis of transcripts of monthly videotapes of mother-child spontaneous interaction in three deaf children spanning the range from 0;9 to 6;0, Launer found consistent periods in the acquisition of derivationally related pairs of nouns and verbs. She found that the children's productions, and also the mothers' signing to children, changed systematically over time. Launer identified the following steps toward acquisition of the formal relations between noun and verb forms.

Period	Age	
1	1–2	Children are simply acquiring lexical items but not morphologically marking related noun and verb forms.
2	2–3	Children sporadically mark nouns and verbs with appropriate features, but do not do so systematically, often providing noncanonical or idiosyncratic markings.
3	3–5	Children now mark full morphological distinctions between nouns and verbs quite systematically, and go on to make overextensions of the formal markings to unpaired forms and to lexical innovations.

Period 1.   Before the age of two, the children's signs do not include the morphological markings that distinguish related nouns and verbs (across 80 percent of cases); children at this early period are in fact primarily learning the parameters of root forms and are not yet distinguishing morphologically related forms. More surprising was Launer's finding that the mothers uniformly and consistently obliterated the distinctions she herself was seeking to classify; but they did so only when signing to children under the age of two years, *not* to older children. For example, a deaf mother was with her two children, ages one and three. To the older child, she signed, "PLEASE YOU GET HER BOOK," making the noun form canonically—with small restrained duplicated movement. Then she handed the book to the younger child and signed "THAT *BOOK" ('That's a book') with large continuous repeated movements, without any of the featural properties that mark the noun. Mothers' productions to children younger than two tended to exaggerate sign size and to repeat the sign form many times, but in the process they sometimes produced forms with dynamic characteristics not found in ASL signs and without the required derivational distinctions. (Both mothers' and children's productions

were judged *ungrammatical* by deaf adults.) Was the difference made because the mothers surmised that their young children, like older non-native signers, might not be ready for the finer distinctions? We cannot be sure; certainly it is not the case that enlarging a sign form extinguishes its morphological marking automatically, since, in signing from a stage or across distances, there is a general enlargement of signs but with preservation of morphological markers. Figure 2–5*B* shows the noun sign AIRPLANE, an enlarged "stage" version of the noun form, and an example of a "noun" form used by mothers in Period 1 children. The "motherese" is neither noun nor verb, nor is it a possible adult form; rather, it is a distortion that obliterates morphological markings.

In mother-to-child signing at this early period, we also found occasional mimetic elaborations of signs, signing on the children's bodies, or molding the children's hands. Mothers sometimes elaborated the image basis of signs to these very young children (only 8 per cent of the signs in a sample were so elaborated, but about 20 per cent of the formationally related noun-verb pairs were). For example, the sign DUCK, which has an image base of the opening and closing of the beak of a duck, was signed to a child under two years old with an enlarged opening and closing movement going toward the child and ending in a playful gentle "bite" on the child. After age two, the mother-to-child signing changed dramatically; sequences were longer, mimetic elaborations and exaggerated repetitions dropped out, and mothers provided the morphological features that mark the distinctions between noun and verb forms in the adult language. Thus, during this first period of lexical acquisiton, children do not formally distinguish ASL nouns and verbs.

Period 2.   The children sporadically mark nouns and verbs with the appropriate set of feature markings, but they do not do so systematically (only 20 per cent of the time are the full distinctions present). In general, during this period, children are learning the privileges of occurrence of nouns and verbs and their syntactic use in sentences, but they have not yet mastered the systematic movement features that differentiate them in the adult language. There are many instances of related nouns and verbs used in the same, or in consecutive utterances; but most do not have the full morphological markers. Nearly half the time, children provide *other* distinctions between nouns and verbs that are not part of the movement featural markers; for example, they change the movement direction, speed, or shape of one of the members or add facial or bodily distinguishers. These are what Launer has termed noncanonical distinctions. Sometimes these are idiosyncratic, as when a child signs KEY with unidirectional movement and the related verb form LOCK with bidirectional movement. Thus, before the morphological distinctions (marked by layered features of movement) are consistently used by the children, they sometimes use redundant or even idiosyncratic markings to distinguish a noun from a verb, as though there is a growing awareness of the distinction in ASL; but they have not yet mastered the appropriate featural markers.

Period 3. Launer found that deaf children between three and four years of age were providing the morphological markers quite consistently, and, even by the following year, extending them to new forms. At this period the markers were applied *across the board* to signs, regardless of their mimetic or iconic bases, and regardless of whether they represented concrete objects and activities or whether they represented more abstract nouns and verbs. Iconicity thus has neither a facilitative nor a hindering effect on the generalization of a morphological process. Figure 2–6*A* shows the child signing the noun DOOR and the verb OPEN-DOOR with the appropriate morphological markings. Cases with no distinctions have virtually disappeared, and most nouns and verbs are marked with full or partial featural distinctions (70 per cent).[5]

The children during Period 3 begin marking nouns and related verbs differentially in earnest in the same way that adults do in citation form. At this period there are even related sentences in which both members of the pair occur with full marking. For instance, one child, age 3;4, was signing about plans for a trip to see her grandmother. "LATER HAVE AIRPLANE, WILL FLY," she signed ("We will have an airplane and fly in it"). Another child of age 3;6 invented a story in which she had an imaginary car that she did not want to drive. "Here's the key," she signed to her mother, handing her an imaginary key: "YOU DRIVE MY CAR" (Fig. 2–6B). The child used the single root of DRIVE and CAR but differentiated the two forms by their full morphological markers. These three year old children, then, were systematically distinguishing noun and verb forms within a single sentence.

The most striking evidence that children have analyzed out morphological markings from across sign forms differentiating noun and verb classes is that they extended these markings to new instances in a variety of ways:

Nouns	Verbs
CLOTHESPIN (3;11)	BUILD-HOUSE (3;2)
TYPEWRITER-KEYS (4;4)	PUSH-WHEELBARROW (3;7)
LAMB (4;4)	LIGHTER-ON (3;8)
JAIL (4;9)	TO-PICNIC (4;4)

Figure 2-6. Derivational relationship between noun and verb. *A,B,* Child's correct signs; *C,* overextension.

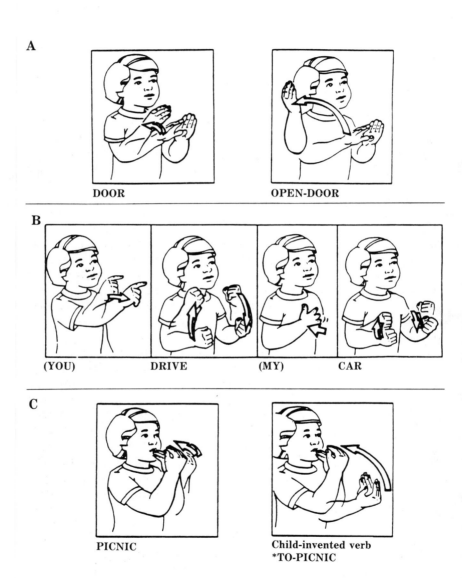

A

DOOR   OPEN-DOOR

B

(YOU)   DRIVE   (MY)   CAR

C

PICNIC   Child-invented verb
                *TO-PICNIC

Some children invented signs and provided the appropriate morphological markers, as in invented signs for LAMB, TYPEWRITER-KEYS, BUILD-HOUSE. Some children extended forms in the language to invent partners or to regularize exceptions. One child extended the ASL noun sign PICNIC which does not have a related verb and, using an appropriate verb marker, signed something like "to picnic" (Fig. 2–6C). Another child was complaining about her mother's control of her activities, and signed the equivalent of "Home is like a jail. I can't open the door, I can't go out. I'm put-in-jail," using the single movement form for the verb. The adult ASL noun and verb form JAIL/PUT-IN-JAIL are identical, the distinction perhaps having been neutralized. However, in the child's signing, the two instances of JAIL (one a verb and one a noun) were marked differentially. The verb conformed to adult usage; however, the child unexpectedly provided the iconical marker (restrained manner, small size, repeated movement) for the noun as an over-regularization.

One child invented her own mimetically based form CLOTHESPIN, with an image based on pinning something on a clothesline. An imitation of the mimed act would have a single closing and release of the clothespin as it is attached to the line. The child's form instead had the nonmimetic (repeated, restrained, small) movement characteristic of nouns. Thus, even here in an invented sign where the mimetic aspects of the movement of a form might be expected to prevail, those aspects gave way to the nonmimetic: the child extended the morphological markers across all forms.

We have examined herein three of the first morphological systems of ASL to be mastered by the signing child. Because of the transparency of forms, we surmised that these would be systems in which a profound influence of iconicity might be expected. What we found, however, was that the transparency at all levels appears to have little or no effect, and that the deaf child systematically analyzes out discrete morphological components of the system presented to him or her in an ordered and orderly fashion.[6] The evidence suggests that the course of acquisition of ASL is startlingly like that of spoken languages of a similar structural type. In details of timing and the nature of errors, the process appears to be more like the acquisition of Hebrew than of Turkish (Berman, 1982, and personal communication; Slobin and Aksu, 1980). In ASL, morphological markers are not affixal, are nonsegmental, and are nonstressable; moreover, they are simultaneously organized with the sign root. The fact that the articulators in sign language are visible and manipulable could provide a special route to learning; mothers, in fact, mold and shape young children's signing. Our evidence shows that this, too, is steadfastly and systematically ignored by the signing children who firmly hold their ground and stay with their incorrect analysis until they themselves arrive at a reorganization of their language system.

THE INTEGRATION OF SYSTEMS: SPATIALLY ORGANIZED SYNTAX

We have shown that, despite the difference in modality, the course of acquisition of sign language is remarkably like that of the acquisition of various spoken languages. There is, however, one area in which the mastery of the system appears to come at a surprisingly late period— surprising in that it involves not only aspects of pronominal reference and the verb agreement system but also the integration of these into a spatially organized referential framework for syntax and discourse. In the future, studies of the development of the mechanisms underlying such functions in deaf children may give us a powerful new tool for investigating the acquisition of discourse organization in languages in general.

Languages have different ways of marking grammatical relations among lexical items. In English, such relations are signaled largely by the order of items; in other languages these relations are signaled by case marking or verb agreement morphology. All of these rely, at some level, on linear ordering of words or segments. By contrast, in a visual-spatial language like American Sign Language, relations among signs are stipulated primarily by manipulation of points in space. A horizontal plane in front of the signer's torso plays an important role in the structure of the language; nominals introduced into the discourse are associated with specific points in the plane of signing space. Pointing to a specific locus later in the discourse clearly refers back to a specific nominal, even after many intervening signs. Indexable verbs are obligatorily marked for person (and number) via such spatial indices, which specify subjects and objects of the verb. Coreferential nominals must be indexed to the same locus point to maintain identity (Bellugi and Klima, 1982; Padden, 1983). Thus, the same signs, in the same order but with a change in direction of movement of the verb, indicate different grammatical relationships. Furthermore, meaning can be preserved under a different temporal order, since relationships are specified spatially. The system of spatial indexing permits relative freedom of word order (in simple sentences, anyway) and yet provides a clear specification of grammatical relations by spatial means. The use of space in these different systems (pronominal reference, nominal establishment, verb agreement, maintaining identity of loci, spatial contexts) is complex and dynamic. In each subsystem there is a mediation between the visual-spatial mode in which the language has developed and the overlaid grammatical constraints in the language. Thus, the syntax and discourse of American Sign Language rely heavily on manipulations of abstract points in space and of spatial representation. This difference in surface form of grammatical mechanisms could have important consequences for the acquisition of sign language.

In our laboratory, Loew has begun a study of deaf children's spontaneous narratives and is examining the acquisition of the systems underlying anaphoric reference (Loew, 1982). We find the following stages in acquisition in the signing child:

At age 3;1, the child's storytelling is extremely difficult to understand, owing in large part to unclear reference. Signs follow one after another with no use of space and without syntactic indicators of which characters performed which actions. Verbs are rarely indexed for nonpresent reference; and, if they are, they are indexed without explicitly associating nominals with the indices. It is important to note that, as we described above, the same verbs are consistently and correctly indexed for present reference at this age. Thus, it is clear that the two systems (verb agreement and establishment of nominals) are functionally separate systems for the child. At this age, the child's formal mechanisms for conveying anaphoric reference beyond present contexts are minimal. The child converses freely of matters outside the here and now, and has no problems conceptualizing them; her problems clearly lie in conveying explicit information about them according to the spatialized grammatical mechanisms provided by the language.

At age 3;6, the child begins to make use of indexing in storytelling; however, she does not explicitly establish identities for loci. Furthermore, the child tends to use one locus for several referents, stacking them up at one locus point, thus still leaving reference unclear and ambiguous (Fig. 2–7A). (Petitto, 1983a, describes one child's first use of abstract spatial loci, in which he "stacked" 11 characters in one location!)

At age 4;4, the child uses several different loci in a single story but still does not generally establish identities for loci, nor does she maintain a referent-to-locus mapping. The child seems to mark shifts in character spatially, but does not maintain identities, and she distributes loci randomly.

By 4;9, the child has increased use of indexing and begins to have consistent use of a designated locus for a referent. Storytelling is

Figure 2-7. The acquisition of spatial indexing.

A

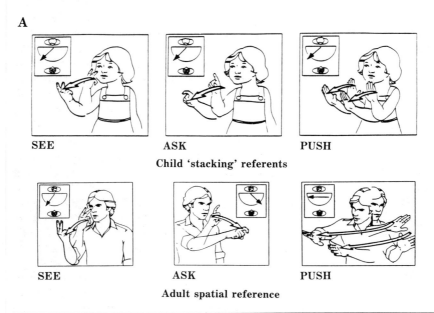

SEE   ASK   PUSH

Child 'stacking' referents

SEE   ASK   PUSH

Adult spatial reference

B

(I)   WANT   MY . . .

YOUR . . .   JANE'S   CHILDREN

qualitatively different from earlier stages and is much more adult-like; the use of space is frequently incorrect, but by this age it is pervasive. The child has begun to integrate various aspects of spatial reference and addressee interaction; loci are now often formally established and used consistently. The child attends closely to the addressee at role transitions, and makes frequent self-corrections at such boundaries, suggesting that she is aware of the possibilities of confusion at these points. Figure 2–7B shows a particularly complex example in which the child was recounting an imaginary story in which she, Jane, had ten children, and another woman arrived to claim them as her own. Jane, when taking the role of the other woman, signed: "(I) WANT MY . . . YOUR . . . JANE'S CHILDREN." She finally resorted, understandably, to the use of her own name sign to clear up reference in this situation!

Analysis of the nature of the child's errors thus clarifies the multileveled character of the reference system. Spatial reference must be used consistently to identify as well as to contrast referents. The child's errors seem to occur at the interfaces of the system and thus draw attention to these interfaces. The study of the acquisition process therefore heightens our understanding of the adult language system.

In this section, we considered the acquisition of a domain in which the nature of the apparatus used in ASL may have its most striking effect: the means by which relations among signs are stipulated in sentences and in discourse. In a spoken language like English, the intended reference of lexical pronouns used by children, and sometimes by adults as well, is often unclear. The spatial mechanisms used in ASL, by contrast, require that identity of referents be maintained across arbitrary points in space, which are not lexical units. In English this is a matter of lack of clarity; in ASL the failure to maintain identity results in strings that are ill formed or judged ungrammatical. Thus, what is required by the grammatical system evolved in this visual-spatial language lays bare the problems the child has in organizing coherent and cohesive discourse.

SUMMARY

The study of language acquisition in deaf children brings into focus some fundamental questions about the human linguistic capacity. In our own research over the past decade, we have been specifying the ways in which the formal properties of languages are shaped by their modalities of expression, sifting properties peculiar to a particular language mode from more general properties common to all languages, and thus reflective of biological determinants of linguistic form. We have described similarities in principles of organization between spoken and sign languages. However, our studies show also that, at all structural levels, the *surface* forms of a sign language are deeply influenced by the modality in which it develops—in the co-occurring layers of lexical, derivational, and inflectional structure, and in the pervasive use of spatially organized syntax. In sign language we can clearly observe the child's acquisition of the spatial mechanisms of the language and the separate structural systems they embody, and these observations can give us a unique viewpoint on the acquisition process across modalities. The specific requirements posed by ASL syntactic spatial mechanisms, for instance, may illuminate problems all children have, hearing or deaf, with maintaining topics and subjects across discourse.

In this chapter, we have examined three of the first morphological systems to emerge and be mastered by deaf children—as well as how these subsystems are integrated into mechanisms for organizing syntax and discourse. In general, it appears that despite the radical differences in modality of language, deaf and hearing children show a dramatically similar course of development, given a natural language input at the critical time. The deaf child, as does his or her hearing counterpart, analyzes out discrete components of the system presented to him or her. Furthermore, the evidence suggests that even when the modality and the language offer possibilities that seem intuitively obvious (pointing for deictic pronominal reference, for example) the deaf child appears to ignore their directness. The comparison of signed and spoken languages will surely become a privileged testing ground for examining iconic, semantic, cognitive, and formal linguistic influences on the course of the acquisition process.

What can we conclude from examining the deaf child's acquisition of the morphological systems considered here? The data show powerfully how language, independent of its transmission mechanisms, emerges in the child in the rapid, patterned, and—above all—*linguistically driven* manner.

ACKNOWLEDGMENTS

This work was supported in part by the National Institutes of Health Grant #NS15175 and #HD13249 and by National Science Foundation Grant #BNS 811479 to the Salk Institute for Biological Studies. Illustrations were drawn by Frank A. Paul.

We are grateful to the deaf children and parents who have taken part in our longitudinal studies of the acquisition of sign language from the onset of first gestures to the mastery of the spatially organized syntax. We are also grateful to the children, teachers, and staff of the California School for the Deaf in Fremont, California, for their spirited participation in these studies, which provide new perspectives on the human capacity for language.

FOOTNOTES:

[1]We use the following notation in this chapter:

SIGN	Words in capital letters represent English labels (glosses) for ASL signs. The gloss represents the meaning of the unmarked, uninflected, unmodulated, form of a sign out of context.
SIGN-SIGN	Multiword glosses connected by hyphens are used where more than one English word is required to translate a single sign, as in LOOK-AT.
(SIGN)	A sign gloss within parentheses indicates that the sign is an indexic sign made with a pointing handshape that changes path of movement and orientation to indicate its referent: (ME), (YOU), (IT), and so forth.
'meaning'	Words within single quotation marks indicate the meaning or referent of the words or signs; for example, 'tree' indicates the referent tree, not the English word *tree*.
SIGN[X:]	A form that has undergone indexical change. The form or meaning may be specified, as in INFORM[X:1 to 2] or INFORM[X:'I to you'].
SIGN[N;M]	A form that has undergone inflection for number and distributional aspect or for temporal aspect, focus, or degree.
SIGN[D:]	A form that has undergone a derivational process.
*SIGN	An asterisk preceding a sign form indicates that it is ungrammatical within adult ASL.
SIGN→	An arrow following a sign form indicates that the sign is held during the course of the subsequent sign.

[2]Our studies suggest that, in the signal, the layers of structure co-occur but are separable, perhaps even composed of different structural components (Bellugi, 1980). For example, deaf signers are highly accurate at recognizing and identifying morphological operations presented in point-light displays, suggesting that these patterns of dynamic contours of movement form a distinct isolable (but co-occurring) layer of structure (Poizner, Bellugi, and Lutes-Driscoll, 1981).

[3]Children's ages are noted in terms of digits referring to years and months (e.g., 2;11).

[4]Meier studied only the acquisition of verb agreement with spatial loci of referents that are present within the context of the conversation. Verb agreement with arbitrary spatial loci that have been associated with nominals introduced into the discourse context requires integration of several subsystems.

[5]After the age of four years, children are also learning optional rules for marking related nouns and verbs in discourse (e.g., deletion of repetition in nouns in lists and in repeated reference). See Launer (1982) for details.

[6]This argument has also been made with respect to the acquisition of another domain of ASL morphology, that of verbs of motion and location which are themselves constructed of morphemes, sometimes labeled as 'mimetic depiction' (Newport, 1981; Newport and Supalla, 1980; Supalla, 1982).

REFERENCES

Aksu, A. A., and Slobin, D. I. (in press). Acquisition of Turkish. In D. I. Slobin (Ed.), *The cross-linguistic study of language acquisition.* Hillsdale, NJ: Lawrence Erlbaum Associates.

Baker, C., and Cokely, D. (1980). *American sign language: A teacher's resource text on grammar and culture.* Silver Spring, MD: National Association of the Deaf.

Bellugi, U. (1980). The structuring of language: Clues from the similarities between signed and spoken language. In U. Bellugi and M. Studdert-Kennedy (Eds.), *Signed and spoken language: Biological constraints on linguistic form* (pp. 115–140). Dahlem Konferenzen. Weinheim/Deerfield Beach, FL: Verlag Chemie.

Bellugi, U., and Klima, E. S. (1979). Language: Perspectives from another modality. In *Brain and Mind* (Ciba Foundation Symposium 69, pp. 99–117). Amsterdam: Excerpta Medica.

Bellugi, U. and Klima, E. S. (1982). From gesture to sign: Deixis in a visual-gestural language. In R. J. Jarvella and W. Klein (Eds.), *Speech, place and action: Studies of language in context* (pp. 297–313). New York: John Wiley & Sons.

Bellugi, U., and Studdert-Kennedy, M. (Eds.) (1980). *Signed and spoken language: Biological constraints on linguistic form.* Dahlem Konferenzen. Weinheim/Deerfield Beach, FL: Verlag Chemie.

Berman, R. (1978). *Modern Hebrew structure*. Tel Aviv: University Publishing Projects.

Berman, R. (1982). Verb-pattern alternation: The interface of morphology syntax, and semantics in Hebrew child language. *Journal of Child Language, 9*, 169–192.

Brown, R. (1980). Why are signed languages easier to learn than spoken languages? In W. C. Stokoe (Ed.), *Proceedings of the first national symposium on sign language research and teaching* (pp. 9–24). Silver Spring, MD: National Association of the Deaf.

Charney, R. (1980). Speech roles and the development of personal pronouns. *Journal of Child Language, 7*, 509–528.

Chiat, S. (1981). Context-specificity and generalization in the acquisition of pronominal distinctions. *Journal of Child Language, 8*, 75–91.

Chiat, S. (1982). If I were you and you were me: The analysis of pronouns in a pronoun-reversing child. *Journal of Child Language, 9*, 359–379.

Clark, E. V. (1977). From gesture to word: On the natural history of deixis in language acquisition. In J. S. Bruner and A. Garson (Eds.), *Human growth and development: Wolfson College lectures, 1976*. Oxford: Oxford University Press.

Deutsch, W., and Pechmann, T. (1978). Ihr, Dir or Mir? On the acquisition of pronouns in German children. *Cognition, 6*, 155–168.

Fischer, S. (1973). Verb inflections in American Sign Language and their acquisition by the deaf child. Paper presented at the Winter Meetings, Linguistic Society of America.

Fischer, S., and Gough, B. (1978). Verbs in American Sign Language. *Sign Language Studies, 18*, 17–48.

Hoffmeister, R. (1978). *The development of demonstrative pronouns, locatives and personal pronouns in the acquisition of American Sign Language by deaf children of deaf parents*. Doctoral dissertation, University of Minnesota.

Jakobson, R. (1979). Shifters, verbal categories and the Russian verb. Russian Language Project, Department of Slavic Languages and Literatures, Harvard University.

Klima, E. S., and Bellugi, U. (1979). *The signs of language*. Cambridge, MA: Harvard University Press.

Lane, H., and Grosjean, F. (Eds.) (1980). *Recent perspectives on American Sign Language*. Hillsdale, NJ: Lawrence Erlbaum.

Launer, P. (1982). *Acquiring the distinction between related nouns and verbs in ASL*. Doctoral Dissertation, City University of New York.

Loew, R. C. (1982). Roles and reference. In F. Caccamise, M. Garretson, and U. Bellugi (Eds.), *Teaching American Sign Language as a second/foreign language* (pp. 40–58). Silver Spring, MD: National Association of the Deaf.

McCarthy, J. (1979). *Formal Problems in Semitic phonology and morphology*. Doctoral dissertation, Massachusetts Institute of Technology.

Meier, R. (1981). Icons and morphemes: Models of the acquisition of verb agreement in ASL. *Papers and Reports on Child Language Development, 20*, 92–99.

Meier R. (1982). *Icons, analogues, and morphemes: The acquisition of verb agreement in American Sign Language*. Doctoral dissertation, University of California, San Diego.

Newport, E. (1981). Constraints on structure: Evidence from American Sign Language and language learning. In W. A. Collins (Ed.), *Minnesota symposium on child psychology*, (Vol. 14). Hillsdale, NJ: Lawrence Erlbaum Associates.

Newport E., and Ashbrook, E. (1977). The emergence of semantic relations in American Sign Language. *Papers and Reports on Child Language Development, 13*, 16–21.

Newport, E., and Supalla, T. (1980). The structuring of language: Clues from the acquisition of signed and spoken language. In U. Bellugi and M. Studdert-Kennedy (Eds.), *Signed and spoken language: Biological constraints on linguistic form* (pp. 187–212). Dahlem Konferenzen. Weinheim/Deerfield Beach, FL: Verlag Chemie.

Padden, C. (1979). Complement structures in American Sign Language. Working paper, University of California, San Diego.

Padden, C. (1981). Some arguments for syntactic patterning in American Sign Language. *Sign Language Studies, 32,* 239–259.

Padden, C. (1982). Syntactic spatial mechanisms. Working paper, The Salk Institute for Biological Studies, La Jolla, CA.

Padden, C. (1983). *Interaction of morphology and syntax in American Sign Language.* Doctoral Dissertation, University of California at San Diego.

Petitto, L. A. (1983a). *From gesture to symbol: The relationship between form and meaning in the acquisition of pesonal pronouns in American Sign Language.* Doctoral dissertation, Harvard University.

Petitto, L. A. (1983b). From gesture to symbol: The relation between form and meaning in the acquisition of ASL. *Papers and Reports on Child Language Development, 22,* 100–107.

Poizner, H., Bellugi, U., and Lutes-Driscoll, V. (1981). Perception of American Sign Language in dynamic point-light displays. *Journal of Experimental Psychology: Human Perception and Performance, 7,* 430–440.

Schwamm, E. (1980). 'More' is 'less': Sign language comprehension in deaf and hearing children. *Journal of Experimental Child Psychology, 29,* 249–263.

Siple, P. (Ed.) (1978). *Understanding language through sign language research.* New York: Academic Press.

Slobin, D. I. (1980). The repeated path between transparency and opacity in language. In U. Bellugi and M. Studdert-Kennedy (Eds.), *Signed and spoken language: Biological constraints on linguistic form* (pp. 229–246). Dahlem Konferenzen. Weinheim/ Deerfield Beach, FL: Verlag Chemie.

Slobin, D. I. (1982). Universal and particular in the acquisition of language. In E. Wanner and L. R. Gleitman (Eds.), *Language acquisition: State of the art* (pp. 128–172). Cambridge, England: Cambridge University Press.

Stokoe, W. C., Casterline, D., and Croneberg, C. G. (1965). *A dictionary of American Sign Language.* Washington, DC: Gallaudet College Press.

Supalla, T. (1982). *Structure and acquisition of verbs of motion and location in American Sign Language.* Doctoral dissertation, University of California, San Diego.

Supalla, T., and Newport, E. (1978). How many seats in a chair? The development of nouns and verbs in American Sign Language. In P. Siple (Ed.), *Understanding language through sign language research* (pp. 91–132). New York: Academic Press.

Wilbur, R. (1979). *American Sign Language and sign structure research and applications.* Baltimore, MD: University Park Press.

Chapter 3

Assessment of Hearing Impaired Children: Determining Typical and Optimal Levels of Performance

Ann E. Geers

For many years, abilities of deaf children were measured in relation to their normal-hearing age mates. A relatively new emphasis in assessment of the hearing impaired is on development of tests that have been designed for and standardized on hearing impaired children. These tests are intended to reflect the deaf child's ability in relation to *typical* hearing impaired children. Examples are the Stanford Achievement Test for the hearing impaired and the test devised by Quigley, Steinkamp, Power, and Jones (Test of Syntactic Abilities, 1978). Moog and Geers recently published a test of English language production, the Grammatical Analysis of Elicited Language (1979), which presents norms for both deaf and hearing children.

For many deaf children it is more informative to define their strengths and weaknesses in relation to other hearing impaired children than in relation to their age mates with normal hearing. With these norms, deaf children who are achieving below the 10th percentile in relation to hearing children may score above the 80th percentile in relation to their deaf age mates. This information is useful in parent counseling and in educational planning. However, the relatively poor performance of deaf children on tests normed on hearing children has led many to conclude that retarded or very limited academic achievement is a necessary result of the condition of deafness. The acceptance of test scores at or above the 50th percentile for deaf children as indicative of adequate progress may lead us to expect too little of these children and to accept as appropriate too little educational effort.

In addition to providing tests and norms that delineate 'typical'' levels of performance for hearing impaired children, there is a need for defining optimal performance levels for these children as well. For many profoundly deaf children, the performance of normal hearing children may be an unrealistically high level of expectation and the performance of so-called typical deaf children may be unrealistically low. In order to evaluate objectively the wide variety of approaches being advocated for educating deaf children today, it is necessary to compare results with both the typical performance and the optimal performance that can be expected of such children.

This chapter reports the results of two studies recently completed at Central Institute for the Deaf. The first examines typical performance of a large number of profoundly deaf children across the country. The second examines optimal performance of a small group of deaf children in an enriched educational setting.

GAEL-S TEST

The data presented first were derived from the standardization of the Grammatical Analysis of Elicited Language—Simple Sentence Level (Moog and Geers, 1979). This test of English language production was initially standardized on normal hearing two to five year olds and hearing impaired five to nine year olds from oral–aural programs. These programs use exclusively spoken English for communication. Publication of the test with these norms for spoken English led to a number of requests for additional norms for children from total communication programs, where signed English is used simultaneously with spoken English in the education of the deaf child. Data were subsequently collected from children in total communication programs and their performance was compared with that of the oral–aural sample.

The test instrument used to elicit and score the language samples was the Grammatical Analysis of Elicited Language–Simple Sentence Level (GAEL-S). The GAEL-S consists of a set of 21 games and activities, which were specifically contrived to elicit a total of 94 target sentences exemplifying a variety of early developing simple sentence structures. The procedure ensures that each child's language sample is elicited in precisely the same manner. Activities were developed using a sample of normal hearing four year olds and were refined and modified until each target sentence was reliably elicited in 90 per cent of the pilot sample. The activities include opening boxes, manipulating toys, describing objects, storytelling, and guessing games. In the Toy Manipulation activities, the examiner performs actions with toy figures and asks the child to describe what happened. For example, in one item the examiner makes the Mommy and Daddy dolls walk across the table. The child responds by producing his or her best approximation of the target sentence, "Mommy and daddy walked." Some children might, for example, respond only with "Mommy walk." If this happens, the examiner models the target sentence for the child, saying, or saying and signing, "Mommy and daddy walked." The child then attempts to imitate this sentence as best he or she can, producing, perhaps, "Mommy daddy walk." In the Guessing Games, the examiner and child take turns manipulating toys behind a screen to stimulate questions such as, "What is in the red block?" and "How many airplanes are in the yellow cup?" In the Opening Boxes activities, the examiner and child take turns opening compartments of specially designed boxes to elicit descriptive statements such as, "That is another yellow chair." In Story Telling, picture sequence stories are used to elicit narrative sentences such as "The girl is brushing her hair."

Throughout the test, in addition to producing each target sentence on his or her own, the child is also expected to imitate the same sentence after it is said or said and signed by the examiner. First the child produces the target sentence, or what the examiner considers to be his or her best attempt at that sentence. This is called the child's *prompted production*. Next the examiner says or says and signs the target sentence and then tells the child to say or say and sign it again. This is the child's *imitated production*. The child is given the opportunity to imitate every target sentence, regardless of the level of his or her first production. Thus, every sentence receives a prompted score and an imitated score. The test session is recorded, in our experiment on videotape. The examiner reviews the tape and records the child's deviations from the target sentences on a transcription sheet.

Each target sentence is preanalyzed into its grammatical components on a preprinted score sheet. Errors noted on the transcription sheet are entered into the appropriate grammatical column of the score sheet. The number correct in each column is then determined and constitutes the score for that category.

The GAEL transcription is scored in terms of grammatical structures. Each of the structures sampled on the GAEL is an early developing form. For example, all structures are rated at level three or below in Lee's Developmental Sentence Analysis (1974), indicating that they appear early in the spontaneous speech of normal hearing children. The test contains 56 articles, 28 adjectives, 17 quantifiers, 8 possessives, 6 demonstratives, 6 conjunctions, 47 pronouns, 58 subject nouns, 56 object nouns, 15 Wh-questions words, 54 verbs, 50 verb inflections, 42 copulas, 42 copula inflections, 29 prepositions, and 8 negatives.

Children were tested at 20 oral–aural (OA) programs and 15 total communication(TC) programs across the country. Only children who met the following criteria were included in the sample:

1. Chronological age between 5 years 0 months and 8 years 11 months.

2. Hearing loss (average of 500, 1000, and 2000 Hz) in the better ear greater than 90 dB.

3. Educated with a consistent communication approach (whether oral or TC) since the age of three years.

4. No additional handicaps of educational significance.

The number of children in each of the four age groups is shown in Table 3–1.

A total of 327 children were included in the sample, 168 from oral programs and 159 from total communication programs. The children were evenly distributed between oral and TC within each age group. Average hearing loss was 103 dB in the better ear for both the oral and TC groups.

All children were tested by teachers of the deaf who had been extensively trained in GAEL administration procedures. All of the children in total communication programs were tested by the same examiner who, as the child of deaf parents, has been a skilled signer for many years.

All of the TC programs included in the sample describe their manual system as "signed English." This means that the word order and inflectional system maintains English structure. Before testing the TC children, the examiner reviewed the sign system used by a particular program with teachers in that school so that the vocabulary and inflectional system used in the test were those familiar to the children. Since the GAEL is a test of English language skills, use of American Sign Language (ASL) was not assessed.

All test sessions were videotaped, and the child's productions were transcribed and scored according to standard GAEL procedures. Productions of children using total communication were scored in three ways. First a transcription was made only of the child's signed production, then another transcription was made of the child's spoken production, and a final transcription was made of the child's combined signed and spoken production. In the combined transcription a structure was counted as correct if it was correct in either the signed or the spoken mode.

TABLE 3-1. Distribution of Subjects

Age Group	Oral-Aural	Total Communication	Total
5	37	37	74
6	38	34	72
7	48	46	94
8	45	42	87
Total	168	159	327

TABLE 3-2. Test–Retest Reliability
(GAEL-S)

Prompted	Educational Program	Imitated	Test Mode
0.96	Oral-Aural	0.96	Oral
0.92	Total Communication	0.75	Oral
0.94	Total Communication	0.91	Manual

Per cent correct scores were obtained for each grammatical category and averaged across all 16 categories to obtain an overall per cent correct score for each transcription. Test–retest reliability was examined for a subsample of 20 oral and 20 TC children to whom the GAEL-S was readministered by a staff member at their own school after a two month interval. Reliability coefficients, presented in Table 3–2, exceed 0.9 for all modalities except the imitated oral productions of TC children, for which the coefficient was 0.75.

Results for the entire sample were summarized first by age group and then by grammatical category. The total score for prompted productions is plotted in Figure 3–1 for each of the four age groups for each of the four communications modes: oral production of children enrolled in oral-aural programs (filled circles), manual productions of children enrolled in total communication programs (filled triangles), oral productions of TC children (open circles), and combined productions of TC children (open squares).

An analysis of variance by age and communication mode showed significant overall effects of each of these variables, with no significant interaction effects. A Duncan's multiple range test revealed no significant difference between the performance of five and six year olds or between seven and eight year olds, but there was a significant increase in scores

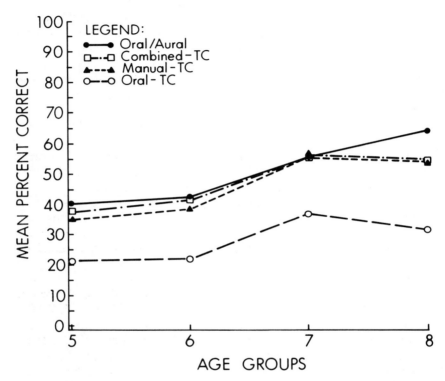

Figure 3–1. Mean per cent correct GAEL-S prompted productions averaged across all grammatical categories are plotted for four age groups in four communications modes: oral productions of children in OA programs, combined productions of children in TC programs, manual productions of children in TC programs, and oral productions of children in TC programs.

from the five and six year old groups to the seven and eight year old groups. No significant differences were found among oral productions of orally educated children, signed productions of TC children, and combined productions of TC children at any age group. However. the oral productions of TC children were significantly below those of all other modes at all age groups.

A similar pattern is reflected in Figure 3–2, in which per cent correct for imitated productions is plotted. As would be expected, children imitated a higher percentage of these structures than they produced on their own, but no change in the pattern of significant differences from the prompted productions was observed.

In Figure 3–3 per cent correct scores for prompted productions are presented for each of the 16 grammatical categories averaged across all age groups. As before, the oral productions of children using oral communication are plotted with filled circles, the manual productions of TC children by filled triangles, and the oral productions of TC children by open circles. The combined scores of the TC group have been eliminated to simplify the graph, since they are virtually identical to the manual scores.

The oral productions of TC children are significantly below their manual productions and below the oral productions of orally educated children in all grammatical categories. The graph has been divided into three segments to depict differences between the oral productions of the oral–aural sample and the manual productions of the TC sample.

The nine grammatical categories plotted in the lefthand section of Figure 3–3 are those in which children educated orally obtained significantly higher scores than the manual scores of children educated in total communication: subject nouns, object nouns, verbs, possessives, adjectives, quantifiers, articles, pronouns, and demonstratives. In four categories (Wh-questions, prepositions, conjunctions, and verb inflections), there were no significant differences between signing scores of TC children and scores of orally educated children. In three grammatical categories (negatives, copulas, and copula inflections), in the righthand section of the figure, the manual productions of TC children significantly exceeded the oral productions of orally educated children.

Results for imitated productions appear in Figure 3–4. As was the case for prompted productions, oral productions of TC children fall significantly below those of the other modalities. The productions of orally educated children significantly exceeded the manual productions of TC children in ten grammatical categories. In six categories there was no significant difference in the imitated productions of these two groups. Only in the category of copula verbs did the TC children imitate signs significantly better than orally educated children imitated speech.

Thus, although average per cent correct scores across all grammatical categories show no significant difference between signing skills of TC children and spoken language of orally educated children, analysis by grammatical category reveals significantly higher scores of the oral group in over half of the grammatical categories, whereas the TC group obtained significantly higher scores in less than 20 per cent of the categories.

One finding of this research that can be expected to arouse comment among educators of deaf children is the considerable gap between the

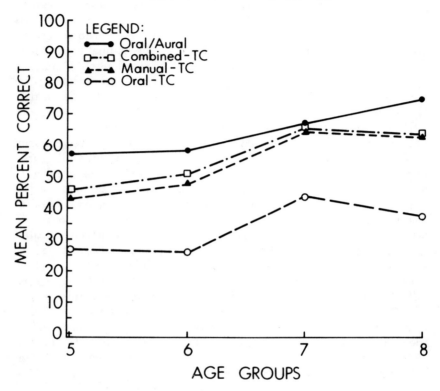

Figure 3–2. Mean per cent correct GAEL-S imitated productions averaged across all grammatical categories are plotted for four age groups in four communication modes: oral productions of children in OA programs, combined productions of children in TC programs, manual productions of children in TC programs, and oral productions of children in TC programs.

oral and manual productions of children educated in total communication programs. It has been somewhat widely claimed that children taught in programs using combined spoken and signed English would spontaneously acquire both modalities at about equal rates, and would acquire competence with English faster than those taught in programs not using signs (Gerber and Prutting, 1981; Moores, 1978; Quigley, 1969; Sperling, 1978). The assumption has been that the use of signs would

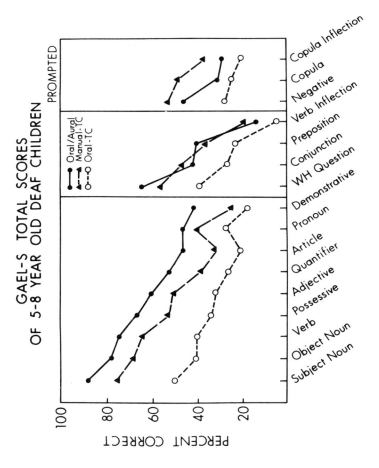

Figure 3-3. Mean per cent correct GAEL-S prompted productions averaged across all age groups are plotted for each grammatical category in three communication modes: oral productions of children in OA programs, manual productions of children in TC programs, and oral productions of children in TC programs.

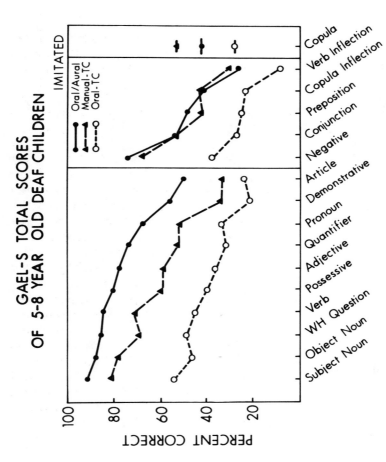

Figure 3–4. Mean per cent correct GAEL-S imitated productions averaged across all age groups are plotted for each grammatical category in three communication modes: oral productions of children in OA programs, manual productions of children in TC programs, and oral productions of children in TC programs.

facilitate the development of spoken English. However, the gap between the oral and manual productions of children in total communication programs indicates that in actual practice spoken English does not develop simultaneously with signed English and that children educated in programs using signed English do not develop competence with English at a rate faster than those not using signs.

Another, perhaps even more important, finding for those responsible for educating deaf children is the degree to which the productions of all of these children reflect their limited facility with English. Both groups of children, ranging in age from five to nine years old, scored far behind normal hearing four year olds.

The task of this GAEL test required children to produce such sentences as "Mommy jumped over the yellow chair," "What is in the red block?" and "Daddy pushed the big bed." The longest sentence was "The boy pushed the yellow chair to the table" (nine words); and the most difficult sentence was "Is the dog in the boy's chair?" Normal hearing children produce all of the sentences sampled in the GAEL-S easily by four years of age. The only categories on which deaf children in our sample obtained scores of 70 per cent or higher in any modality were nouns, verbs, and Wh-question words. These are the high information carrying words, which do allow a child to express himself or herself in a telegraphic manner. These categories alone, however, do not provide a sufficient basis for the child to successfully master the important task of learning to read and write English.

In both the OA the TC programs, however, there were some children who were acquiring English skills well and who did, in fact, demonstrate mastery of the structures sampled on the GAEL-S. Twenty-six children from OA programs and ten children from TC programs achieved 85 per cent or higher overall scores. This means that it is possible for profoundly deaf children to acquire these structures and that some of them are able to develop facility with English at the levels evaluated. However, for the majority of the children in our sample, this potential is not being realized. Careful and intensive teaching techniques must be developed to pull the performance of more deaf children above the average or typical level represented here.

EPIC PROJECT

It would appear that, rather than relying on the method of communication to alleviate the significant problems imposed by early profound deafness, the answer lies in improving the quality of teaching.

The following question has gnawed at us for many years: Can "typical" deaf children achieve well above what is generally expected, even approaching the achievement of hearing children, with improved teaching? Our attempt to answer this question was EPIC, the Experimental Program in Instructional Concentration (Calvert, 1981), a three year project that combined efforts of the school and research staff at Central Institute of the Deaf (CID).

The school staff was charged with designing an ideal program for elementary school–aged deaf children, and was given unlimited money, staff, materials, and space. The research staff was charged with measuring the effectiveness of this newly designed educational program. A description of the program appears in *American Annals of the Deaf* (Calvert, 1981). This chapter focuses on the evaluation study and its results.

In the fall of 1978, all severely and profoundly hearing impaired children between six and eight years of age who could be considered "typical" deaf children in that they did not demonstrate significant learning problems in addition to their hearing loss, were selected from the CID population. These 16 children were to spend the next three years in an intensive educational program designed to accelerate their development in all areas.

In addition to the intensification of the curriculum, the program included reduced pupil–teacher ratio (2.3 children to each teacher), homogeneous grouping that varied from subject to subject depending on the skill level of the children, and increased parental involvement in out-of-school educational activities.

The need for a control group was apparent from the beginning, but a year was spent in selecting the most appropriate comparison. Ideally this group would have been selected from CID, since the educational program in the rest of the school represented the "norm," which we hoped to exceed. However, all children in the required age group who met the criteria were already enrolled in the experimental group. The alternative solution was to select children from other programs that were as similar to CID as possible.

Two other private oral schools for the deaf agreed to participate by providing comparison children, who were similar to the EPIC group at pretest in age, hearing loss, and overall ability. Twelve children at one school and nine at the other met the criteria for inclusion in the project and were pretested in the fall of 1979.

Posttest data were collected twice—once after two years and again after a third year. Comparative results from both groups at the two year posttest are published in *American Annals of the Deaf* (Calvert,

1981). The third year posttest results are reported for the experimental group only. Since third year posttesting was finally conducted on the control group last spring, results from comparisons of these groups over a three year time span can now be reported. During the three year period of this project, one child in the experimental group moved away from St. Louis and three children left the comparison school programs; so the final number for the project was 15 children in the experimental group and 28 in the control sample.

At the beginning of the project, both groups ranged in age from 6 years 1 month to 8 years 11 months. The mean age was 7 years 6 months for the control group and 7 years 3 months for the experimental group. The control group had slightly better hearing (99 dB as opposed to 103 dB in the experimental group) and significantly higher mean nonverbal IQ (115 in the control group as opposed to 105 in the experimental group) (Wechsler, 1974). The investigators realized from the beginning that any intensification devised would need to have a dramatic impact in order to show a significant improvement over the performance of this control group. Children in both groups were producing simple sentence structures on the GAEL-S (Moog and Geers, 1979) at a considerably higher level than other seven year olds in oral education programs across the country, as shown in the Figure 3–5A. The lowest dashed line represents the oral norm for deaf seven year olds. The dotted line represents the control group at pretest; the children are at the 61st percentile in relation to other deaf seven year olds. The experimental group, represented by the solid line, are at the 69th percentile.

By the end of the first two years of the project, shown in Figure 3–5B, both groups are so near the top of the GAEL-S that it no longer provides a sensitive measure of the differences between these groups. At an average age of 9 years, 0 months, these children are still having trouble with verb inflections, but all of the other categories appear to be well developed. Therefore, this test was not repeated at the end of the third year.

The entire battery of tests selected to evaluate children in the EPIC project is described and summarized in Calvert's report (1981). There were three tests of spoken expressive language, seven tests of receptive spoken language, one test of expressive written language, one test of receptive written language, two tests of speech intelligibility, two tests of speech perception (one lipreading alone and one auditory alone), two tests of reading, and a test of academic achievement. All of these tests were administered at pretest and again after two school years had elapsed. A smaller battery of tests was selected to be administered at

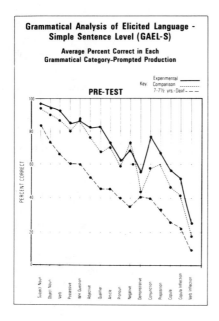
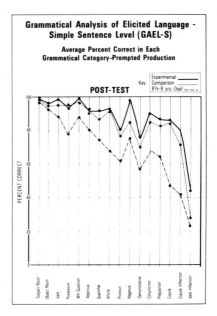

Figure 3–5. Average per cent correct prompted productions in each of the 16 grammatical categories of the GAEL-S are plotted in the graph on the left for three groups: the standardization sample of deaf seven to seven and a half year olds, the EPIC control group at pretest, and the EPIC experimental group at pretest. In the graph on the right, average per cent correct prompted productions in each of the 16 grammatical categories of the GAEL-S are plotted for three groups: the standardization sample of deaf eight and a half to nine year olds, the EPIC control group at two years posttest, and the EPIC experimental group at two years posttest.

the end of the third school year. Test instruments which were selected for the third year battery were those with a sufficiently high ceiling to continue reflecting progress.

The abbreviated battery of tests is presented in Table 3–3 along with mean scores obtained by the experimental and comparison groups at the three test periods. The first column of Table 3–3 lists the skill areas evaluated; the second column, the evaluation measures used; and the third column, the type of score reported. The fourth column lists the mean scores of the control group at pretest (fall of 1979) followed by the two year posttest in the spring of 1981 and the three year posttest

TABLE 3-3. EPIC Evaluation Results—Average Scores of Experimental and Control Groups

Skill Area	Evaluation Measure	Score Type	Control Group			Experimental Group		
			Pretest	2nd Year Posttest	3rd Year Posttest	Pretest	2nd Year Posttest	3rd Year Posttest
	Chronologic Age		7–6	9–2	10–2	7–3	8–11	9–11
Hearing	Audiogram	BE SFA	99			103		
Intelligence	WISC-R	PIQ		115*			105	
		VIQ		69			75	
Language	Peabody Picture Vocabulary Test	Age	3–6	4–4	4–9	3–11*	5–1	6–2†
	ITPA							
	Auditory Association	Age	4–0	5–4	6–0	4–0	6–3*	7–7†
	Grammatic Closure		2–5	4–2	5–4	2–5	4–8	6–3†
	NSST							
	Receptive	% Correct	50	65	69	58†	69	81†
	Expressive	% Correct	29	38	46	40	51*	62†
	Test of Syntactic Abilities	% Correct	—	53	55	—	68	74†
	Grammatical Analysis of Written Language	DSS	1.0	4.2	6.9	2.1	6.1*	10.7†
Speech	Intelligibility	% Intelligibility	38	56	58	43	70*	85†
Academics	American School Achievement Test	Grade Score						
	Sentence/Word Meaning		2.0	3.0	3.3	2.0	3.1	3.9†
	Paragraph Meaning		1.9	2.6	3.5	1.8	2.8	4.1
	Arithmetic Comp.		1.7	3.2	3.9	1.7	3.3	4.4
	Arithmetic Prob.		1.7	2.4	3.1	1.9	2.6	3.4

* P ≤ .05
† P ≤ .01

in the spring of 1982. The last three columns contain mean scores of the experimental group at pretest in the fall of 1978 followed by results at the two posttest periods. Tests of statistical significance were used to compare scores of the experimental and control groups at each test period. Scores marked with an asterisk or dagger are those that are significantly higher than scores obtained by the other group at that test period.

At pretest the experimental group scored significantly higher than the control group on two measures. Two years later, the experimental group scored significantly higher on 4 of the 13 measures and at the end of the third school year they scored significantly higher on 10 of the 13 measures.

The Peabody Picture Vocabulary Test (Dunn, 1965) is a measure of single word receptive vocabulary standardized on normal hearing two to 18 year olds. The child's task is to select the picture named by the examiner from a choice of four. The control group progressed from an age score of 3 years 6 months at pretest to a score of 4 years 9 months three years later. Mean age score of the experimental group went from 3 years 11 months to 6 years 2 months for a significantly higher score at posttest.

In Figure 3–6, mean vocabulary age scores are plotted against mean CA over the three test sessions for the experimental (solid line) and control (dashed line) groups. The line of best fit to each set of data points is also plotted, and the slope of each of these functions appears at the end of each line. The slope for normal hearing children (not plotted here) is 1.0—one year's vocabulary gain for each year's gain in chronological age. The experimental group is progressing at 0.82 of a year in vocabulary for each year's age gain, whereas the control group is progressing at less than half the normal rate.

Another test that produces age scores over a relatively broad age range (from two to ten year olds) is the Illinois Test of Psycholinguistic Abilities (ITPA) (Kirk, McCarthy, and Kirk, 1968). Two subtests were selected from this battery to evaluate the acquisition of vocabulary and certain types of grammatical structures.

The Auditory Association subtest consists of a series of 42 analogies presented to the child verbally, such as "grass is green, snow is _____." The vocabulary becomes more difficult as the task progresses.

Results over the three-year period are plotted in Figure 3–7. The experimental group progressed at a rate slightly better than normal, proceeding from the four year level to the seven and a half year level in less than three years. The control group progressed at about three fourths of the normal rate.

PEABODY PICTURE VOCABULARY TEST

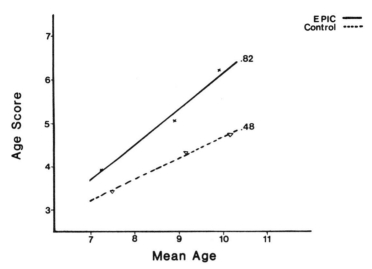

Figure 3-6. Average Peabody Picture Vocabulary Test age scores are plotted against mean chronological age at three test periods for experimental and control group children.

ITPA – Auditory Association

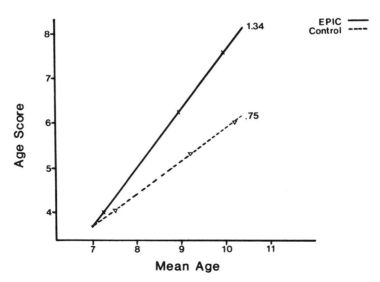

Figure 3-7. Average ITPA Auditory Association subtest age scores are plotted against mean chronological age at three test periods for experimental and control group children.

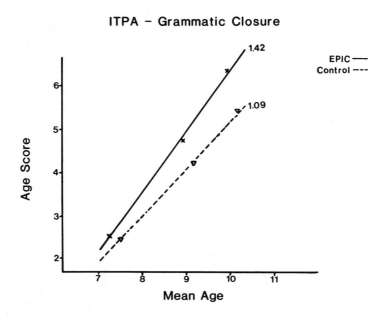

Figure 3–8. Average ITPA Grammatic Closure subtest age scores are plotted against mean chronological age at three test periods for experimental and control group children.

The Grammatic Closure subtest consists of a series of 33 pictures about which the examiner says a sentence followed by one to be completed by the child with the correct word or grammatical inflection (e.g., "The boy had two bananas. He gave one away and kept one for _____)." Results are plotted in Figure 3–8. On this subtest the progress for both groups was as good or better than normal. Both groups started out at the bottom of this test (the two and a half year level). but the experimental group ended up about one year ahead of the control group.

The Northwestern Syntax Screening Test (NSST) (Lee, 1971) is intended to screen both receptive and expressive language abilities of normal hearing children three to eight years. The test primarily samples the child's use of prepositional phrases, negatives, and subject-verb agreement. Since there is no direct transformation of raw scores to

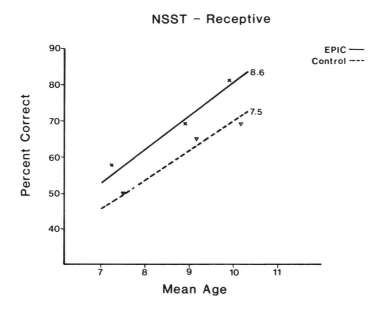

Figure 3-9. Average per cent correct receptive scores on the NSST are plotted against mean chronological age at three test periods for experimental and control group children.

age scores, results are expressed in terms of per cent correct. The slopes, therefore, cannot be used to compare rate of development with that of normal hearing children. They can be used, however, to examine rate of progress in children in experimental and control groups. Results of the receptive portion of the NSST are presented in Figure 3-9. The experimental group shows a slope of 8.6 with a mean score of 81 per cent correct at the end of three school years. The control group slope was 7.5 with a posttest score of 69 per cent.

Expressive scores are plotted in Figure 3-10. The slope for the experimental group is 8.4, with a mean score of 62 per cent at posttest, while the control group gained 7.5 points per year for a final score of 46 per cent correct.

The Screening Test of the Test of Syntactic Abilities (TSA) (Quigley et al., 1978) was administered to assess each child's ability to recognize correct forms of written standard English syntax. Since meaningful results require a minimum of third grade reading level, the TSA was administered only at the last two test periods. Per cent correct scores averaged across all nine grammatical categories are presented in Figure 3-11. The control group shows negligible growth over a year's time

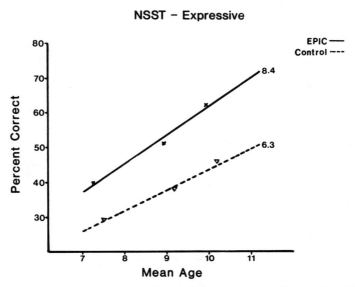

Figure 3–10. Average per cent correct expressive scores on the NSST are plotted against mean chronological age at three test periods for experimental and control group children.

and achieves a score of 55 per cent correct at the end of the project. This is similar to the performance of the deaf normative sample tested by Quigley and associates (1978), who averaged 53 per cent across the 10 to 18 year range, and those reported by Moeller and colleagues (1981), for another sample of nine and a half to 20 year old deaf children (56 per cent). The experimental group, however, does show improvement with age for an overall posttest score of 74 per cent correct. This performance is particularly impressive since their average age at posttest is 9 years 11 months, which is younger than any children tested in the studies by Quigley and Moeller and their colleagues.

Our measure of written language, the Grammatical Analysis of Written Language (GAWL), was devised specifically for this project, so the scores can be meaningfully compared only between the experimental group and control group. Written language samples were evaluated in terms of the grammatical maturity of sentences spontaneously generated by children in relating a simple story.

The Developmental Sentence scoring system (DSS) (Lee, 1974) was used for scoring the written samples. In this system 1 to 8 points are awarded for levels of complexity of usage of various grammatical structures. These points are added for each sentence, and the score represents the mean number of points per sentence. Mean DSS points

TEST OF SYNTACTIC ABILITIES

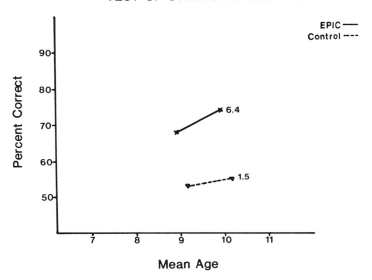

Figure 3–11. Average per cent correct scores across nine grammatical categories of the Test of Syntactic Abilities Screening are plotted against mean chronological age at two test periods for experimental and control group children.

for each group are plotted in Figure 3–12. At the beginning of the project the groups produced very little written language. However, the control group gained over 2 developmental sentence points per year, and the experimental group gained over 3 points per year so that by age 10 the control group's mean score was almost 7 and the experimental group's almost 11.

To evaluate Speech Intelligibility each child's production of 10 simple sentences was recorded and played to 16 listeners, who wrote down what they heard. These responses were scored according to a procedure described by Monsen (1978). These scores are plotted in Figure 3–13. The slope of the improvement function for the experimental group is almost twice that observed in the control group. Thus, by the end of the project, children in the experimental group averaged 85 per cent speech intelligibility compared to 58 per cent in the control group.

Academic grade level for reading and mathematics were evaluated with the American School Achievement Test (Pratt, Stouffer, and Yanuzzi, 1975). The only significant difference between these groups is the third year scores of the experimental group in Sentence and Word Meaning.

WRITTEN LANGUAGE

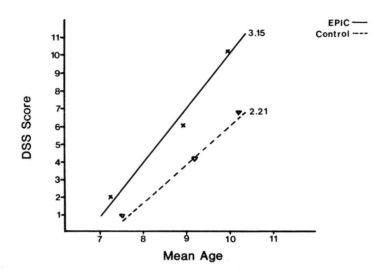

Figure 3–12. Average Developmental Sentence Scores on the GAWL are plotted against mean chronological age at three test periods for experimental and control group children.

Since reading is an area for which considerable comparative data are available, these results may be compared with those of other studies of deaf children reported in the literature. In Figure 3–14, reading grade scores of a variety of samples from deaf children at different ages are plotted with a line of best fit extrapolated to estimate reading grade level of each of the groups at age 13. The portions of the slopes based on real data are indicated by a solid line and extrapolated portions are shown by a dashed line.

The topmost function (filled circles) illustrates the reading growth expected from an average group of normal hearing children who have an expected growth of one grade level per year, which results in a grade level of 8.0 by age 13.

The lowermost function (open squares) was plotted from average reading scores on the Stanford Achievement Test from the Office of Demographic Studies' nationwide Annual Survey of Hearing-Impaired Children and Youth (1971). The line of best fit for these data has a slope of 0.10 grade level per year for an average reading grade level of 2.4 by age 13 years. The next highest function (open circles) is plotted from a cross section of deaf children, 11 to 13 years old, in 73 school programs in the United States and Canada, summarized by Wrightstone, Aranow,

SPEECH INTELLIGIBILITY

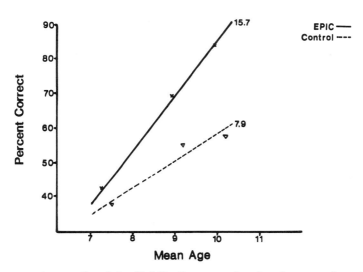

Figure 3-13. Average Speech Intelligibility Scores are plotted against mean chronological age at three test periods for experimental and control group children.

and Muskowitz (1963). The line of best fit for these data has a slope of 0.21 grade level per year for an average reading grade level of 3.1 by age 13.

The next highest function (open triangles), represents scores of 11, 12, and 13 year old children at CID on the American School Achievement Test reported by Lane and Baker (1974). This slope of 0.41 grade level per year results in an average reading grade level of 4.4 by age 13. Data from the EPIC control group are represented in the next highest function (inverted triangles) with a slope of 0.48 grade level per year, which extrapolates to a reading grade level of 4.8 by age 13. Data for the EPIC experimental group are represented in the next highest function (x's). This group of children showed growth in reading scores of 0.73 grade level per year, which extrapolates to a grade level of 6.3 by age 13.

The results of the EPIC study suggest to us that although the achievement of these deaf children continues to lag behind that of their normal hearing age mates, there is no evidence that it reaches asymptote or a constant plateau from which it does not recover regardless of teaching time or effort. Rather, in all areas of achievement for which we tested the children, in both the control and experimental groups, they continued to learn as long as they were taught.

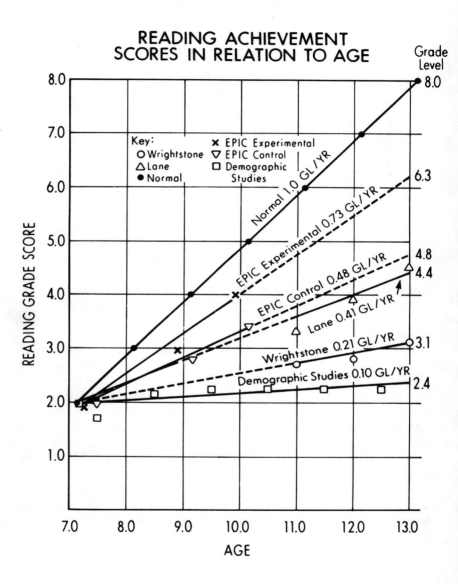

Figure 3–14. The rate of growth in reading achievement grade scores with age is depicted by drawing a line of best fit to scores obtained from normal-hearing children, the EPIC experimental and control groups, Lane and Baker (1974), Wrightstone and associates (1963), and the *Annual Survey of Hearing-Impaired Children and Youth* (1971).

Furthermore, children in the experimental group, for whom instructional efforts were intensified, demonstrated a significantly accelerated rate of progress.

These findings have ramifications that are not limited solely to programs that use oral communication exclusively or primarily for teaching deaf children. We believe both the data and the teaching techniques developed in this project can be generalized for use in instructional programs in which total communication, fingerspelling, or signed English are used, provided that the instruction is maintained at an equivalent level of concentration.

In conclusion, it can be suggested that amelioration of the problems of early profound hearing loss has not been found in any one method of communication (be it oral–aural, total, cued speech, acoupedic) or device (be it powerful amplification, cochlear implant, vibrotactile stimulation, and so forth) or educational setting (schools for the deaf, segregated classes, or mainstreaming). All of these methods, devices, and settings have, at one time or another, been proposed as "solutions" to the educational problems presented by deafness.

Such emphasis discounts the most important ingredient in effective education of the deaf child—well-structured educational programs that are based on the realization that most deaf children require extremely careful, intensive, individualized instruction in order to realize their potential.

REFERENCES

Annual Survey of hearing-impaired children and youth: Series D, No. 9, (Spring, 1971). Washington, DC: Office of Demographic Studies, Gallaudet College.

Calvert D. R. (Ed.) (1981). EPIC–Experimental Project in Instructional Concentration. *American Annals of the Deaf, 126*, 8.

Dunn, L. M. (1965). *Peabody picture vocabulary test.* Circle Pines, MN: American Guidance Service.

Gerber, S. E., and Prutting, C. A. (1981), Bilingualism: An environment for the deaf infant. In G. T. Mencher and S. E. Gerber (Eds.), *Early mangement of hearing loss.* New York: Grune & Stratton.

Kirk, S. A., McCarthy, J. J., and Kirk, W. D. (1968). *The Illinois test of psycholinguistic abilities.* Urbana, IL: University of Illinois Press.

Lane H. S., and Baker, D. (1974). Reading achievement of the deaf: Another look. *Volta Review, 76,* 489–499.

Lee, L. (1971). *Northwestern syntax screening test.* Evanston, IL: Northwestern University Press.

Lee, L. (1974). *Developmental sentence analysis.* Evanston, IL: Northwestern University Press.

Moeller, M. P., Osberger, J. J., McConkey, A. J., and Eccarius, M. (1981). Some language skills of the students in a residential school for the deaf. *Journal of the Academy of Rehabilitative Audiology, 14*, 84–111.

Monsen, R. B. (1978). Toward measuring how well hearing-impaired children speak. *Journal of Speech and Hearing Research, 21*, 2.

Moog, J. S., and Geers, A. E. (1979). *Grammatical analysis of elicited language—simple sentence level.* St. Louis: Central Institute for the Deaf.

Moores, D. G. (1978). *Educating the deaf: Psychology, principle and practice.* Boston: Houghton Mifflin.

Pratt, W. E., Stouffer, G. A, and Yanuzzi, J. R. (1975). *American school achievement tests.* Indianapolis: Bobbs-Merrill.

Quigley, S. (1969). *The influence of fingerspelling on the development of language, communication, and educational achievement of deaf children.* Urbana, IL: University of Illinois.

Quigley, S. P., Steinkamp, M. W., Power, D. J., and Jones, B. W. (1978). *Test of syntactic abilities.* Beaverton, OR: Dormac.

Sperling, G. (1978). Future prospects in language and communication for the congenitally deaf. In L. S. Liben (Ed.), *Deaf Children: Developmental perspectives.* New York: Academic Press.

Wechsler, D. (1974). *Wechsler intelligence scale for children—revised.* New York: The Psychological Corporation.

Wrightstone, J. W., Aranow, M. S., and Muskowitz, S. (1963). Developing reading test norms for deaf children. *American Annals of the Deaf, 108*, 311–316.

Section III

EMOTIONAL CONSIDERATIONS

The birth of a child is a profound and moving experience for most parents. The discovery, or even the suspicion, that a new infant is not perfect can be shattering. Moses and Schlesinger both address the issue of parental grief, but from different viewpoints. Moses sensitively reviews the emotional stages of grief—denial, guilt, depression, anger and anxiety—as first identified by Kubler-Ross in terminally ill patients. We become aware that grieving is a universal experience that does not require learning. Moses focuses on the grieving process as it affects the parents of a newly identified hearing impaired child. The professional's dilemma is to reconcile the concept of early intervention with the parents' initial need to deny the diagnosis. Moses discusses the responsibility of professionals to support parental grieving to facilitate the habilitation of the deaf infant.

Schlesinger looks ahead to the effect of unresolved grief on the hearing impaired child's future academic development. She speculates that the educational deficits for the deaf are similar to maladaptive characteristics found in other disadvantaged groups. Schlesinger's theoretical hypothesis is that the underlying problem for deaf persons and other disadvantaged groups is related to a feeling of powerlessness to influence the future. She cautions that parental feelings of incompetence may be related to lack of professional support during the diagnostic process. Parents feel overwhelmed by the child and his deafness. Schlesinger challenges us to encourage parents to interact positively with the child. Coping successfully with the child's disability will return a measure of self-esteem to the parents. Both Moses and Schlesinger stress the importance of an interdisciplinary approach in the management of the deaf child and the family.

Chapter 4

Infant Deafness and Parental Grief: Psychosocial Early Intervention

Kenneth L. Moses

Over the last 10 or 15 years many habilitation and rehabilitation professions concerning themselves with children have become aware that it is not possible to treat a child's sense, function, or limbs in isolation (Friedlander, Sterritt, and Kirk, 1975). Indeed, the tenets of the holistic approach have been generally accepted as the only way to successfully habilitate or rehabilitate children. Working with a child's ears, while ignoring the rest of that child's functions or developmental struggles, seems almost absurd at this time. Professionals have come to recognize the interrelationship between locomotion, vision, hearing, cognition, and social–emotional development and now understand that children, not functions, develop and grow. Such a conceptualization has had two effects upon the fields: it has created interdisciplinary diagnostic and habilitation settings, and it has broadened the training of professionals working with hearing impaired children. Such thinking has been the impetus behind the research and clinical application of the early intervention concept with hearing impaired children. Earlier intervention increases the involvement between professionals and the parents of deaf children.

Unfortunately, not all settings have yet incorporated holistic concepts of how a child develops and what is needed for a child's total habilitation. Professionals have quickly discovered that neither the necessary cooperation nor the attainment of such broad knowledge comes easily. Specifically, one of the areas of repeated concern is related to parent counseling, that is, the interactions between parents and those professionals who are primarily trained to work with their children. Generally, a primary stumbling block for the professional is the emotional states that many parents manifest while trying to deal with the impact of having a deaf child.

Such emotional states are often a manifestation of grieving (Buscaglia, 1975; Gordon, 1975, Kubler-Ross, 1969; Moses, 1977; Stewart, 1978; Webster, 1976).

HEARING IMPAIRMENT, PARENTING, AND GRIEF

In the course of anticipating the birth of a child, parents generate dreams, fantasies, and projections into the future of who or what that child is to be for them. Such dreams are often extremely personal and hold great promise for the *parents'* future. Anticipating the birth of a child is a primitive experience that stirs people deeply. Unfulfilled needs, yearnings for the future, wishes to have deficiencies corrected, and desires to have fantasies maintained are often attached to the child yet to be born. Parents generally are deeply attached to these dreams.

Grief is the process whereby an individual can separate himself or herself from someone or something significant that has been lost. Grieving stimulates a reevaluation of an individual's social, emotional, and philosophical environment. Such shifts often lead to positive values and attitudes. Grieving facilitates growth. Without the ability to grieve, a person cannot separate from a lost person or object and thereby, in essence, "dies" with whatever or whomever is lost. These people lose a present and future orientation and focus only on the past, that is, only on the "good old days" before they sustained the loss. Grieving therefore is the catalyst for growth, for with all growth there is loss. Continuous growth requires successful grieving.

Grieving is a primarily affective or emotional process. The affective states are not epigenetic, that is, they have no specific order; one is not a prerequisite for another, and indeed some can be felt simultaneously. Grieving starts spontaneously and appears to require no learning: the affective states seem to be intrinsic, cross-cultural, and even found in some animals (Lewis and Rosenblum, 1974).

Most parents find disability to be the great spoiler of their dreams and fantasies about who or what their child was to be. Most dreams require an unimpaired child; therefore, the initial diagnosis of disability often marks the point when a cherished and significant dream has been shattered. It is that dream that must be grieved for. Unfortunately, the loss of the dream is such a personal and illusive loss that few people understand the nature of the loss. Indeed, the parents may not understand that it is a dream that has been lost, and therefore they are frequently confused by the grief process that follows.

Successful grieving seems to depend on significant human interactions, that is, a person cannot grieve alone. The support that the parent of an impaired child requires to grieve successfully can come from the professional who is working with the child, as well as from husband or wife, friends, religious group, community, and parent organizations. Unfortunately, many of the cultural injunctions in Western society forbid spontaneous grieving. The affective states associated with the process are often difficult to accept by both the grieving individual and those offering support. Ironically, often the people who are needed to facilitate grief instead discourage it. Rather than accepting the denial, guilt, depression, anger, and anxiety, which are a natural part of the grieving process, those closest to the bereaved individual may view these affective states as psychopathological. They may respond with diagnostic labels, expressions of rejection, or fear. Those wishing to offer support may fail to recognize that each of these affective states serves a specific function that allows the parent to separate from the shattered and cherished dream. The separation then permits generation of new dreams, which incorporate the hearing impairment, thus stimulating the emergence of the coping process. Understanding and accepting the value of the emotional states associated with grieving is crucial for professionals and others, if parents are to grieve successfully.

DENIAL

Denial is perhaps the first affective state seen in the process of grieving. Parents of deaf children deny in a number of different ways: they may reject the diagnosis itself, the permanence of the diagnosis, or the impact of the diagnosis. The parent who has difficulty accepting the diagnosis itself often argues with the professional diagnostician. This is the parent who refuses to accept what the diagnostician offers, thereby creating an atmosphere that can cause the diagnostician either to feel insecure about the accuracy of the diagnosis or to feel some anger towards the parent. In either case, an adversary relationship may result. A polite parent, of course, does not confront the professional with denial but rather simply does not follow through on recommendations or fails to cooperate with attempts to habilitate the child.

Other parents, who are denying the impact of the handicap rather than the diagnosis per se, might seem like ideal parents for a day or otherwise disadvantaged child. Such people in essence say that they do not understand all the to-do about having a deaf child because "what's the big deal?" They might state that they know special education has come along way, that cultural attitudes have shifted, and that additional federal legislation has been enacted that offers support for parents of impaired children and ensures equal rights for handicapped people. Professionals concerned with the field are quite aware that deafness is indeed a "big deal" and that it is likely that these parents are denying its impact.

The process of denial is perhaps the most frustrating one for professionals in the communication disorders field, because all evidence points to the efficacy of early intervention for child habilitation. To the professional, denying parents might appear to be in a nonproductive, passive state, which serves no positive function and often interferes with parental cooperation in early intervention.

Denial is neither a random, purposeless state nor a passive, nonproductive one. Denial serves a distinct and important purpose. For individuals to function within an environment fraught with danger, each person must establish a mechanism that keeps him or her from believing that he or she is in real jeopardy. People cannot live from day to day with the fear of cancer, or death, or dismemberment, or of having an impaired child. Such fears would keep human beings from functioning spontaneously. Therefore, most people have within them a mechanism that makes them feel special and invulnerable to the actual dangers about them. As a consequence, when something unpleasant or ghastly occurs—and many parents of deaf children view having an impaired child as a ghastly event—they are wholly unprepared to deal with it. Parents of impaired children need time to constructively incorporate what has occurred.

That the denial process is not a stagnant state that freezes parents in purposeless immobility would be evident in the comparison of two parents, one whose child was born unimpaired and one whose child was born and identified as deaf. The parent denying the deafness would differ emotionally from the parent of the unimpaired child. Denying parents feel distressed and agitated (often to the point of experiencing sleep difficulties). They commonly are guarded in their interactions with others. These behaviors are a sign that the denial process, far from being passive, is an active process in which much is occurring underneath the surface on the preconscious and unconscious levels. The parent is accumulating information and searching for inner strength even while he or she consciously fends off the reality of what has occurred.

Parents of impaired children use denial to buy the time needed to find the inner (ego) strength and the external mechanisms to deal with the problem. These external mechanisms might include acquiring information, skills, and support from family, friends, organizations, and professionals. If the denial process were assaulted before the parent had the inner strength and the outer mechanism to understand the impact of what had occurred, the parents would collapse emotionally.

For early intervention to employ a holistic approach, the child must be seen within the context of a family unit, which includes the parents. To exclude the parents in the child's habilitation is like ignoring the influence of the child's auditory functioning on his or her cognitive development. Professionals working in early intervention, therefore, must be skilled in recognizing and facilitating the grieving process in parents. In particular, they must find ways not merely to tolerate, but also to accept, parental denial while still offering those services needed directly by the child.

Parents who are denying are not suffering from a deficiency in logic nor usually are they unable to understand what is being presented to them. An early intervention clinician can rest assured that there are many people who are telling the parent that he or she is stupid, destructive, inappropriate, or shirking parental responsibility by denying. Instead, the parent needs someone whose attitude conveys an acceptance that embraces the validity of the parent's denial. The implication for the management or counseling of such parents is to *avoid* countless repetitions of the professional's opinion, which leaves the parent feeling foolish, ignorant, illogical, or stupid. There are few people who are unable to give denying parents what they most need: recognition that the individual is most probably a loving parent who, for good reason, cannot at present engage actively in the child's habilitation.

As an example, a parent brought her five year old child for an initial assessment to a multidisciplinary audiological center. With the support of other professionals, the audiologist determined that the child was profoundly deaf. Upon presenting this information to the mother, the audiologist met with strong resistance. The mother repeatedly claimed that the child could hear her name whispered behind her back. The audiologist decided to have the mother demonstrate this seemingly impossible feat. The clinic was in an old building with wood slatted floors. The mother placed her child on that floor and then stood behind her, and with one stamp of her foot whispered, "Mary." Responding most adequately to the vibration in the floor, the child crisply turned around to her mother with a smile. No explanation of how the floor vibrated to stimulate such a response convinced the mother at that moment that her judgment was incorrect. It indeed turned out to be a most frustrating experience for clinician and parent alike until the battle was relinquished, and the clinician could turn to the mother and say:

> It must be most frustrating for you to hear me presenting something contrary to what you believe. The idea of Mary being deaf seems almost impossible for you to accept. Can you tell me a little bit about what it would mean to you if somehow my assessment were correct?

Although the audiologist's manner of relating did not reverse the denial, it did precipitate a long-standing, positive parent–professional relationship.

It is such a relationship that is as much a cornerstone of a child's habilitation as the actual "hands-on" early intervention techniques.

Since denial affords the parent the opportunity to find the inner strength and the external mechanisms to deal with having a deaf child, the denial ultimately ceases when the parent attains such strengths.

GUILT

Guilt, as an affective state associated with grieving, generally is the most disconcerting of the grief states for both the parent and the professional confronting it. Parents of deaf children might manifest guilt in one of three general ways. The first is shown by parents who have actual stories documenting that they indeed have caused their child's handicap. Such stories often involve the taking of drugs during pregnancy, having hidden known genetic disorders in the family, having contracted an avoidable disease, or other such occurrences that the parents believed were within their control. This first manifestation of guilt is the most logical and the least common. Because of its logical nature it seems the least difficult to accept by the professional, although it still is disconcerting. The second way in which parents of hearing impaired children might manifest guilt appears less logical. It is reflected in the parents' belief that the impaired child is just or fair punishment for some specific and awful action that they have committed in the past. There need not be any logical connection between the nature of the past transgression and the nature of the impairment. The third manifestation of guilt that is common in parents of deaf children is of a de facto philosophical nature. This is reflected in the parent who basically states, "good things happen to good people; and therefore, bad things happen to bad people." Such a general belief leaves the parent feeling guilty simply because the impairment exists.

It is hard for many professionals to accept that so painful and debilitating an affective state can have any positive, growth-facilitating elements. In the context of grief, guilt is the vehicle that allows parents to reevaluate their existential beliefs. Seemingly persons hold within themselves a personal belief system that acknowledges control over certain events but allows other occurrences to be comfortably attributed to the whims of chance. How and when certain events are defined as "my own fault," whereas other occurrences are attributed to fate, is an individual and internal process. The goal is to develop a system that allows the parent to be comfortable with classifying events as within his or her jurisdiction of control, or outside of it. It permits the parent, in effect, to avoid the absurdity of assuming full responsibility for all life events, and the equally absurd position of disclaiming any responsibility. The guilt that parents of deaf children experience precipitates their reevaluating the parameters of their accountability.

The case of a young couple exemplifies the issues concerning guilt. Both spouses worked. When their first baby was conceived, the husband encouraged his wife to stop teaching. He argued that she worked with children who often become ill. He went on to say that women in his family never worked when pregnant. His wife argued that she felt fine and saw no reason to discontinue her work, especially since her work tenure and her pregnancy term coincided.

She continued to work and was unfortunate enough to be one of the mothers who contracted rubella during an epidemic. When telling her story she plaintively presented the idea that she had caused her child's handicap. Her child indeed was born deaf and brain damaged as a result of maternal rubella.

It is most tempting for professionals to try to explain to such a mother that her exposure to rubella was unpredictable, that she could as easily have contracted rubella from her next door neighbor's child. But logic is as ineffectual with guilt as it is with denial. Professionals in early intervention need to be aware that guilt does not yield to argument, cajoling, coercing, or even irrefutable scientific evidence. This mother's logical system was as viable as that of the professional, but within a different context. She might well have countered that her husband had accurately predicted what would happen if she continued working.

For guilt to be effective in helping an individual sort out why he or she has an impaired child, the guilt feelings must be shared with an empathetic, significant other person. The professional who fulfills such a role might do so by offering acceptance through an attitudinal framework exemplified by the following possible response: "If you truly believe that you caused your child's hearing impairment, no wonder you feel so badly. Tell me more about it." The prevailing temptation on the part of most professionals is to try to take away the guilt. Indeed, many other people will be attempting to argue with the parents and "fix" the unfixable feeling. It will be the very exceptional person who is able to validate the legitimacy of the parent's feeling without seeming to confirm his or her judgment of fault. To offer such a relationship is to offer a unique opportunity that facilitates growth.

Nothing will make the guilt run its course more quickly than it needs to. There are some factors, however, that can perpetuate this difficult phase. A significant other person is what can make the difference. If the professional can accept guilt as part of a normal, necessary, and facilitative process of grief, the parent will detect the acceptance and will likely engage in a more substantial and ultimately constructive relationship with the professional. By contrast, the professional who views guilt as psychopathology, or who has a condescending attitude toward parents who manifest guilt, will impair the relationship between the parent and the professional. As guilt becomes a successful vehicle for the reexamination of the parent's existential values, it will cease on its own.

Incidentally, the manner in which the parent manifests guilt often reflects the nature of the particular handicap. Many parents of deaf children feel that their child's disability is a specific punishment in the area of communication (Mindel and Vernon, 1971). Again, it is the empathic professional who can offer the most to a parent presenting such a feeling. There is nothing to be cured or fixed. There is only an affective state to be facilitated.

DEPRESSION

In Western culture, interestingly depression is almost always seen as psychopathological. Although it is one of the affective states most commonly identified with grief, most professionals approach a depressed individual as one who must be treated with special deference and care. Unfortunately, such attitudes are usually contradictory to what is needed by the parent who is depressed because of grieving brought on by the impact of having a deaf child.

Depression is defined as anger turned inward, that is, anger toward oneself. This simple definition is generally accepted clinically, although the causes, dynamics, and characteristics of various depressions are obviously far more complex than such a definition might convey. Nonetheless, this definition is useful in understanding depression as a grief state. It might be asked, "For what reason are parents of hearing impaired children angry with themselves?" The answer to such a question leads into the area of potency versus impotency or competency versus incompetency.

Parents can view their potency as existing somewhere between two extreme points: that they were impotent to prevent whatever occurred to their child and feel anger toward themselves for their "useless, impotent state"; or that they were potent enough to have prevented what occurred, and therefore are self-enraged that they did not act before it was too late.

In the face of a negative and permanent occurrence, adults in this culture are forced to reevaluate the nature of their potency and competence. Their personal definitions of self value and productivity become threatened. Depression is a vehicle that encourages this reevaluation. Depressed people view themselves as impotent, incompetent, incapable, and of little value, since they have had little or no impact on something so close them—something that they want so very much to change.

In one case, a woman who dramatically exemplified the dynamics of depression had always been the mainstay and strength of her family. She had been through many struggles and had emerged as the support of everyone around her. She was widowed fairly early in life and left to raise her only son. At age eight the son became seriously ill with a kidney disease that required the risky use of a potentially ototoxic drug. Unfortunately, he was deafened overnight. Months after this occurrence, this woman developed severe depression. As it was an uncommon effective state for her to manifest, the family became alarmed and alerted the professionals who were connected with her son.

On being interviewed, the woman stated that she felt broken, that there was nothing left within her, and that she was impotent to heal the affliction in the most significant person in her life. She felt incompetent and incapable. The temptation to argue against such feelings is powerful. The professional often wished to point out to the parent how much she could do for her child, that indeed she was the mainstay and center of her child's habilitation. Although such statements may be true, they did not fit the mother's perception of her situation. To feel capable, potent, and competent, this parent needed to feel that she could make her child "normal" once again. This, evidently, was impossible, and therefore she saw herself as a failure.

It takes special strength for a professional to sit down with a parent who feels such depression and invite him or her to share in detail the ways in which he or she feels incompetent. The professional might create this facilitative atmosphere by sharing an attitude exemplified by the following statement: "Could you tell me more about the impossible demand that you feel imposed upon you?" Indeed, the mother just described found that such an atmosphere enabled her to reassess her family image of being "the strong one," and to see how that image only increased the pressure she felt. From that vantage point, she was able to reassess her capabilities and also the attitudes of significant people around her. The feelings of depression eventually became feelings that facilitated personal growth.

It is at that point that the input from the professional made a difference. Depressed people do not need cheering up. They do not need someone to implicitly or explicitly deny them the right to feel depression. Instead, they need someone who will allow them to experience their legitimate depression and someone to talk with them about how impotent they feel. Unfortunately, most professionals were taught to relate to depressed people in ways that inadvertently leave them feeling misunderstood, stupid, crazy, inappropriate, or destructive as well as depressed. Depression is part of a normal, necessary, and self-sufficient process of grieving that allows parents to separate from the dreams and fantasies that they have generated around their child. There is indeed value in "wallowing in self-pity," and "crying over spilled milk." What constitutes reality for each individual is reality *as he or she perceives it*; life truly is "as bad as he or she thinks it is."

As parents are permitted to experience depression within an environment of acceptance, they will likely reevaluate how they define competency. Such redefinition permits self-acceptance in spite of not being able to "fix their child." Again, it is the significant other who can offer the atmosphere facilitating this facet of grief.

ANGER

Anger (or rage) is an integral part of grieving. Each person has an internalized concept of justice that permits him or her to move within society without undue anxiety or fear of being mistreated. Such a conception is flexible and changes with maturity. An unpredictable event, such as having an impaired child, threatens the feelings of security around such a belief system. Whenever an individual's sensibilities about order and fairness are disrupted, frustration results. Frustration, agitation, aggravation, irritation, and annoyance are all words that parents of impaired children find on their lips at one time or another, along with anger and rage. Long ago, psychologists noted that frustration leads to aggressive feelings. The parent who is frustrated by the birth of an impaired child feels anger toward the deaf child who has intruded upon his or her life and has disrupted it in many realms. It is expensive, embarrassing, time-consuming, energy-consuming, exposing, and shattering to have a hearing impaired child in the family. On a more psychologically primitive level, most parents feel that all this disruption and pain have emanated from the child.

Since anger toward their child is considered heinous by most parents, they often displace these feelings upon others: spouses, the deaf child's siblings, and, of course, professionals. Such displacement is most unfortunate, since parents are in need of support from the very people whom they may be alienating through their anger. As an alternative, parents may direct their anger and feelings of having suffered an injustice toward God, science, or "the general order of things" or into the fertile areas concerned with oral–aural versus total communication method controversies. This type of displacement can usually elicit empathic understanding more easily from the people around them; yet it also prevents the parents from confronting the real root of their anger, their feelings toward the deaf child.

A note of caution here. Professionals are ordinary human beings capable of error. Indeed, there are some professionals in the habilitation fields whose own personal motives prompt them to behave insensitively or malevolently. Parental anger generated under such circumstances is appropriate and has little to do with the anger that is part of grieving. Thus, not all parental anger represents displacement. It is the anger that has no basis in reality or the prolonged maintenance of anger associated with a justified circumstance that prompts a professional to become suspicious.

The function of anger within the grieving process is that it allows the parent to reassess and reconstruct the internal conception of justice that has been disrupted by the birth of a deaf infant. The parent needs to maintain an internalized sense of justice in the face of this traumatic occurrence. Anger, like the other affective states of grieving, serves a positive role in parental growth. The development of an internal sense of justice changes with maturity. What a teenager sees as being fair versus the more flexible and complex view of justice often held by a person in his or her forties is an example. If the parent of an impaired child is able to incorporate the seemingly unfair circumstance of "having an impaired child without just cause," then he or she will have generated a new internal sense of justice that will permit competent coping with any future losses. Crisis and its concomitant disruption (in this case anger against injustice) provide the impetus for attitudinal changes that foster competency. The more that internal sense of justice is based on reality, the more likely that life's unpredictable occurrences can be handled with competence.

Since it is crucial for the parents to recognize and deal with the anger they feel toward their impaired child, professionals can help by accepting and relating to the anger presented to them. This is difficult; parents who are manifesting feelings of injustice in a general fashion are usually more easily accepted by professionals than are parents who express feelings of anger toward their children. Such professionals have often chosen the habilitation fields because of their sensitivities and humanitarian attitudes toward people with special problems. Many professionals become quite attached to the children they work with and, indeed, recognize how illogical it is for parents to be angry at their deaf children for having disrupted their lives. Nonetheless, this anger appears to be both a common feeling and one that facilitates the grief process. Professionals who offer parents the opportunity to talk openly about their angry feelings toward their children are providing a kind of support that the parent rarely encounters.

Unfortunately, professionals typically are affected most profoundly by an angry parent, and they may act in ways that do not aid the grieving process. Reactions on the part of the professional often depend upon his or her own self-confidence. The more confident professional may become annoyed with the angry parent, sometimes countering with his or her own anger. In contrast, the less secure professional can become quite easily frightened by the angry parent and question his or her own competency, since the parent appears so dissatisfied. In either case the professional is unable to provide the response to parental anger that would facilitate the grief process.

A description of one particular parent can serve as a good example of the anger engendered through grieving. The father, a technician in the electronics field, himself suffered from a moderate handicap (not related to audition). He knew the suffering that it had caused for both him and his parents. As fate might have it, he fathered two children who had hearing impairments that required numerous interventions (surgeries, therapies, special education, and prostheses) from various professions. The cause of the impairment was genetic in nature. This father, along with his wife, held having a large family as a primary value. It was clear that the financial pressures he was already suffering, because of services required by his first two children, prohibited having more children. The blunt financial reality—another hearing impaired child would bankrupt him—was a very disagreeable prospect for this proud and competent man. As he saw it, life had dealt him a triple blow: by giving him a handicap, by giving him "bad" genes that caused him to have handicapped children, and by depriving him of having the large family of which he had dreamed.

He became irascible, critical, demanding, and generally resistive toward "habilitation" professionals. School personnel feared him, and medical professionals fought with him. Parent–professional communications that included this man were strained at best. In a group experience, which he had reluctantly decided to attend, he began to actively criticize and attack the group facilitator (after having passively resisted any and all issues for the first half of the process). He detailed all the reasons why he considered such a group to be useless and also stated all the reasons why he thought the facilitator could offer very little. He went on to say that he resented participating in an "obvious waste of time," and that he, for one, was going to file a complaint against the facilitator to the administration. When the group leader invited him to share more of his feelings by asking him if he felt cheated, and if so, how he generally dealt with feelings of being cheated, the conversation became animated and ultimately moved into the realm of disability, fathering children, and his life dilemma. That conversation stimulated discussions about fairness and justice that moved other people to talk about their feelings of being cheated.

This father did not change radically through exploring and discussing his feelings, but he continued to meet with the group and never filed a complaint. Ultimately, he successfully adopted two more children. In talking with the group facilitator years later, he shared (with humor) that his adoptions were his way of "beating the system"—as he put it, "you can't keep a good man down." He also shared that he no longer felt indiscriminate anger, but that he had channeled it in such a fashion as to become moderately effective in influencing local legislators to back legislation that facilitated the handicapped *and their families!* It was obvious that this man had grown to have a remarkably different internal sense of justice. His anger had prompted change.

It is the professional who will be able to recognize that parental anger is part of grieving and as such warrants acceptance and facilitation. Yet if the professional can tolerate the displacement of anger or the parent's talking negatively about the child, such an interaction would be facilitative. Parents who are able to talk with significant others about their anger are less likely to become abusive parents. Abuse, incidentally, can range from overprotection (denial of the existence of anger) to extrapunitiveness within a socially acceptable context (for instance, the parent who structures an almost inhumane environment for work on language development, taking up every waking hour of the child's life).

If anger is allowed expression, if it is seen as acceptable, if indeed it is incorporated as part of the normal process of grieving, parents of deaf children will come to use the affective state of anger to restructure their internal sense of justice and thereby will move to yet another effective realm.

ANXIETY

Generalized feelings of anxiety are shown by parents who are grieving the loss of a dream because of impaired children. This anxiety is related to the question of how to balance responsibility for the welfare of another human being with the right to have and independent life of one's own. This balance requires a most personal and internal adjustment. The event of having a deaf child disrupts this internal adjustment.

Parents often report shock and dismay at being their child's medical manager. The child seems so vulnerable; the professionals often send messages that imply emergency; there are conflictual messages. There is so much to be learned, and so much seems to hinge on learning it properly. These new pressures and responsibilities are heaped on the already existing pressures and responsibilities of daily existence.

A parent once aptly described this state of grieving as juggling an overwhelming number of precious glass balls. The feelings of responsibility are awesome, and the temptations of becoming a professional parent of a deaf child are strong. Opposed to this is the alternative temptation to run away and then feel terrible guilt and pressure for not having acted constructively. These presses and pulls cause great anxiety. Of course, the attitudes of professionals and other parents with hearing impaired children can strongly influence the amount of pressure that a given parent feels and the amount of concrete responsibility he or she believes must be assumed. In truth, however, definitions of responsibility are an internal psychological process.

Parents who are experiencing anxiety as part of the grieving process are in need of significant others to accept such feelings. It is not helpful to simply tell a parent to "calm down." This is a period when calming down is not only impossible but also maladaptive; for the anxiety itself facilitates a restructuring of the individuals attitudes concerning responsibility. It is, therefore, a time when realistic expectations need to be clearly spelled out, along with an understanding that parents have lives beyond their hearing impaired children. Furthermore, an unwillingness to do certain habilitative activities is acceptable and does not emplify destructiveness or lack of caring. An overstressed, overwhelmed parent ends up doing nothing, even while appearing to be intensely involved in doing everything. A parent who can build space to minister to himself or herself and grant self-permission to skip or reject certain aspects of the habilitative process will be more effective in the long run to facilitate his or her child's growth. A professional's overzealousness to save the child will frustrate the parent's ability to resolve the anxiety phase of grieving.

GRIEF COUNSELING

Grieving, as described, is an affective process that permits the parent of a deaf child to separate from the dreams and fantasies that the parent cherished for the child. The inability to separate successfully from such a dream is devastating to both parent and child. If the parent does not generate new dreams that the child can fulfill, each day the child will be viewed as a disappointment and failure in the eyes of the parent. Parental disappointment will be communicated to the child, leaving the child feeling as though he or she is indeed a disappointment and a source of pain to the parents. If, however, the parent is able to separate from the dream, there is the distinct possibility that he or she will accept the child for what the child actually is. Acceptance is such an important prerequisite of attachment and emotional development that the concept of facilitating grief becomes an important tool to the intervention and habilitation of very young hearing impaired children.

It is the role of the significant other, a role that can be fulfilled by a professional, that can facilitate or frustrate the normal grieving process. Professionals who have negative opinions or difficulty with the affective states of denial, guilt, depression, anger, and anxiety are likely to inhibit the grief process and be detrimental to the habilitation of the child. The professional who is able to convey an attitude of acceptance toward such affective states will have a positive effect upon the parents and help create a sense of security for the child. Without this, children cannot go on to develop in other areas (for example, language) that are seen as tantamount to the successful habilitation of a deaf child.

There is no point in becoming "a grief diagnostician," since the affective states previously described do not go in any order, nor are they mutually exclusive. That is to say, people feel what they feel when they feel it, and they often have two or more feelings simultaneously. Also, an attitude of acceptance aimed at facilitating grief would be damaged by an attempt at diagnosing a person's grief state, since diagnosing is by definition the process of labeling.

The grieving process is far from a one-time occurrence. Parents of deaf children repeat and rework the affective states associated with grieving. Each time the child comes to a major life milestone that impacts on the parent in a new way, grief will be experienced once again. There are certain specific times when many parents seem to feel the impact of the handicap in a new fashion. Obviously, all parents seem to experience it at the point of initial diagnosis. Common developmental points when grieving reoccurs are as follows: (1) when the child reaches "regular" school age (for that is a time when much comparison between children goes on): (2) when the child becomes pubescent (and offers all the dilemmas that puberty generally offers plus the complexities of a handicapping condition): (3) when the child reaches the age of high school graduation (and the disability may negatively affect his or her ability to move on in a more independent manner of functioning); (4) when the child comes to an age when the expectation is that he or she would live totally independently (working on his or her own, getting married, and so forth); and (5) when the parents come to retirement age (and the nature of the disability is such that the child's needs might interfere with the parents retirement and require that arrangements be made beyond the lives of the parents). Success with earlier grieving facilitates later grieving. Also, each new process of grief brings new insights and new strengths not previously realized.

COPING

Since grieving is almost entirely affective or emotional, it is clear that there are other processes that occur simultaneously. The general rubric of "coping" covers most of the remaining activities that require interaction between the parent, the child, the environment, and the systems that serve the child. Although much has been written on the coping process since 1960, the most succinct and clear descriptions and definitions of the process were offered by a rehabilitation psychologist (Wright,1960). In her book, which focuses on the psychological processes of disability, Wright highlighted four major coping processes. Each of these impacts on the parents in such a manner as to precipitate a change in their value system. The four coping mechanisms are as follows: containing the disability effects, devaluing physique, enlarging one's scope of values, and converting from comparative values to asset values.

When parents first begin to deal with the impact of having a deaf child, their tendency is to generalize the effects of the disability. They are prone to see the entire life of the child (and often their own lives) as ruined. It is not uncommon for parents to say things like: "My child will never marry," "My child will never work," or "My child will be dependent on me for the rest of my life." They fear the worst, and then they deal with this as reality. Confrontation with reality is facilitated through the process that prompts an individual to contain the effects of the disability. Such containment is done attitudinally; that is, the parent does not permit the concept of disability to contaminate those aspects of the child that need not be (nor are they) affected by the deafness. The professional can be extremely helpful during this facet of coping by offering as clear and concise an assessment as possible. In particular, one part of the assessment should emphasize the competencies and assets that are not affected by the disability. Parents who can be exposed to deaf adults are also helped with this coping process.

The devaluing of physique, as a coping mechanism, attacks one of the more painful blocks to successfully dealing with handicapping conditions. Western culture places a high value on appearance, often judging people according to what is seen. Unfortunately, most handicapping conditions are seen as ugly. Specifically, "deaf speech," hearing aids, sign language, and behaviors specific to deafness are often viewed negatively. The coping mechanism of devaluing physique deals with this issue. "Physique" is broadly defined here as any detectable manifestation of the disability that might be judged negatively. The issue of physique has seemingly been successfully coped with when a value system has been adopted that focuses on those qualities and competencies we associate with being human, and when the value system ignores or devalues surface qualities.

Enlarging the scope of values works on the premise that most people narrow their value system, experiences, interests, and associations as they age. This appears to be true for a great many people. Such narrowing poses a special problem for parents of a deaf child whose disability precludes their participation in the particular confined life style that they have chosen. If that is so, then to cope, thereby facilitating the child's growth, the parents must be able to enlarge their scope of values enough to genuinely accept whatever life style their child might pursue. Such an exploration requires parents to examine their own values, often precipitating discomfort as to what constitutes "the good life." If such coping does not occur, then both the parents and the child will feel as though the child's life style is second-rate and unacceptable.

The last coping mechanism involves the issues of comparison and competition. Western culture seems to put an enormous amount of emphasis upon winning, doing better than the next person, and comparing one person's performance to another. Although such a comparative atmosphere can be uncomfortable for many nonimpaired people, it is devastating to the impaired individual and his or her family. The parent must come to understand that how an individual succeeds compared with others is far less relevant than the mastery of a skill or the demonstration of a competency. In the fields of hearing impairment, it is interesting to note that there are many measures of a comparative nature concerned with reading levels. Far less evident are measures—or even notations in reports—that speak to how the child uses reading skills to enhance his or her everyday life.

The attitudes fostering these different views toward reading reflect substantively different value systems. The former emphasizes comparative values, the latter, asset values. Ultimately, to cope with the child's deafness, the parent comes to value the child as he or she is, respecting each new achievement as an asset, without comparison to other children. It is through such coping that the parent comes to appreciate primarily the child and focus on the handicap secondarily.

REFERENCES

Buscaglia, L. (1975). *The disabled and their parents: A counselling challenge*. Thorofare, NJ: Charles B. Slack.

Friedlander, B. Z., Sterritt, G. M., and Kirk, S. G. (Eds.) (1975). *Exceptional infant— assessment and intervention*. New York: Brunner/Mazel.

Gordon, S. (1975). *Living fully: A guide for young people with a handicap, their parents, their teachers, and professionals*. New York: John Day.

Kubler-Ross, E. (1969). *On death and dying*. New York: Macmillan.

Lewis, M., and Rosenblum, L. A. (1974). *The effect of the infant on its caregiver*. New York: John Wiley and Sons.

Mindel, E., and Vernon, M. (1971). They grow in silence. The deaf child and its family. Silver Spring, MD: *National Association of the Deaf*.

Moses, K. (1977). Effects of developmental disability on parenting. In M. Rieff (Ed.), *Patterns of emotional growth in the developmentally disabled child*. Morton Grove, IL: Julia S. Molloy Education Centre.

Stewart, J. C. (1978). *Counselling parents of exceptional children*. Columbus, OH: Charles E. Merrill.

Webster, E. J. (1976). *Professional approaches with parents of handicapped children*. Springfield, IL: Charles C Thomas.

Wright, B. A. (1960). *Physical disability: A psychological approach*. New York: Harper and Row.

Chapter 5

Deafness, Mental Health, and Language

Hilde S. Schlesinger

The maladaptive patterns of deaf children and adults are not unique to the deaf but are shared by a number of disparate groups, particularly a large segment of the disadvantaged poor. Large-scale research studies have shown that certain characteristics are common to both many deaf people and many poor individuals, including academic retardation, immaturity, impulsivity, spatial versus temporal orientation, attention to the here and now rather than to the future, and restricted vocational achievement (Altshuler, 1964; Altshuler, Deming, Vollenweider, Rainer, and Tendler, 1976; Auletta, 1982; Levine, 1956; Greenspan, 1980; Sadock, Kaplan, Freedman, and Sussman, 1975).

We are postulating that these similarities are engendered by specific parental experiences and psychological stances and are mediated through certain linguistic styles of caregivers, especially in the toddler years. These linguistic styles appear to encourage toddlers to use language in a way that leads them to develop maladaptive motivational stances, especially during their travels through school systems. We believe that there is a common factor underlying the maladaptive patterns frequently associated with deafness and poverty—a sense of powerlessness.

POWERLESSNESS AND DEFICITS IN LEARNING

What is powerlessness? Power is an operational, theoretical construct related to the sense of having the competence, ability, and opportunity to influence and shape the environment. Powerlessness, then, is the absence of this quality. Powerlessness, directly or indirectly, influences the capacity to learn, the motivation to learn or to demonstrate the fruits of knowledge, and other components of the theory we have developed. An interesting anecdote from the author's experiences in Germany illustrates this point.

It has quite often been said that black children cannot, or choose not to, learn "standard" phonological English, although they are exposed to it frequently and at great length. When military personnel were stationed in Europe, those who learned Bavarian dialect best were black soldiers. This related to a time in Germany when being black was very advantageous. Black American jazz musicians were very popular, the dollar was worth four marks 20, and German girls wanted to marry black soldiers. As a result these American soldiers, who most likely had been exposed to much less Bavarian than to "formal English," learned Bavarian German quite well and quickly. The point here, of course, is that a sense of power can radically modify peoples' desires to acquire and utilize linguistic skills.

A parallel exists from the field of deafness. It is usually said that deaf children's language skills, reading, and language arts appear to improve little during the school years. *After* they leave the school environment, however, young deaf adults develop spurts of acquiring very specific language structures, such as Wh-questions, negatives, and passivization (Boothe, Lasky and Kricos, 1981). The authors speculate that the subjects' communicative interactions after leaving the school environment were more "frequent, more spontaneous and more demanding . . . than those usually found in classrooms." These young deaf adults may also have seen themselves as more powerful than they had been in the classroom situations, which are frequently didactic and nonresponsive. Power thus appears to play a role in learning and may play a role in other dynamics found among the disadvantaged and the deaf. In fact, it has been said that data that social scientists are reporting about the poor are the psychological consequences of powerlessness (Haggstrom, 1964).

Any internal or external variable that diminishes an individual's ability to influence and shape the environment contributes to powerlessness. Obviously, the sense of power is culturally determined and context bound, and thus it is potentially changeable. It appears to be related both to aspirations and to the reality principle. For example, under extraordinary circumstances and for brief periods of time, an individual can perform such herculean tasks as lifting a car. On the other hand, if less and less control over the environment is available to the individual, he or she may tend to withdraw or battle ineffectively. An example of this is found in long-term inmates of displaced person camps, whose every step in life was dictated by others, and who eventually lost competence for self-initiated behaviors. Similarly, victims of burn out develop difficulties with personal accomplishments and experience emotional exhaustion and depersonalization (Meadow, 1980).

The steps leading to the powerlessness experienced by the poor may be obvious. Large numbers of poor people live from crisis to crisis, perpetually attempting to procure the basic necessities of life—money, food, housing, medical care, and employment. External forces heavily influence the outcome of such crises, and the poor may develop a philosophy of fatalism when they realize that they have little effective power to influence their environment. They may resign themselves passively to their fate or ineffectively rail against it. Disadvantaged mothers seem to "see themselves as powerless, helpless and . . . not able to do anything" to affect the development of their children (Minuchin, Montalvo, Guerney, Fosman, and Schumer, 1967). This same attitude is reflected in a paraprofessional's description of his work with members of the underclass as he bemoans the difficulty of

> . . . preparing people for the real world, concentrating on the development of social skills and work habits among a group of people who often operate outside society, who have often lost self-confidence, have frequently grown up with few positive role models, have scant exposure to the world of work, have low frustration thresholds, and are generally unacquainted with being on time, following orders, saying "Thank you" and "Please."
>
> (Auletta, 1982)

The author has heard similar laments from helpers of "low-functioning, deaf adults."

We believe that parents of deaf children and children with other disabilities are also beset with feelings of powerlessness. Although the sources for the powerlessness differ, it will be noted below that the concomitants may well be the same.

What are the sources of powerlessness among the parents of disabled children? The parents have brought forth a child with a disability that they cannot directly influence. Our clinical observations of parents and helpers of parents are replete with descriptions of interactions with professionals and children that indicate a sense of inadequacy and incompetency vis-à-vis the disability, the child, and the professional helpers (Meadow, 1969; Schlesinger and Meadow, 1972). Although parents do find ways of influencing the outcome of their child's disability, the process is a slow and painful one. The grieving process itself contributes pervasively, especially when not initially resolved. This has been described by many authors (Ross, 1964; Schlesinger and Meadow, 1972) and was most recently sensitively discussed by Moses and Hecke-Wulatin (1978). A lack of support by professionals during the diagnostic crisis, followed later by "professional" advice that is seen as overwhelming, conflicting, or incompatible, that frequently revives sorrow and fear, or that seems to usurp the parents' right to know or to decide, can all contribute to stress and often lead to crises in parenting (Schlesinger, 1976). Features of their deaf child's lack of responsiveness to sound or lack of understanding for some parents may revive potent ghosts from the nursery. These may be seen as rejection, exclusion, secrets, or simply as not being understood, and thus contribute to parental perplexity. Having borne a deaf infant may tug at a parent's self-esteem for many years.

Power is a central component of several of the major criteria of mental health delineated by Coopersmith (1967), particularly mastery of the environment, autonomy, and self-esteem. Thus, the powerlessness of the parents may be transmitted to the children and to the caregivers of the children. It is also said that the parents elicit feelings of powerlessness as well in intervention agents, who, for example, tend to speak of working "on" rather than "with" such families (Durning, 1980). Such an environment may then influence the overall mental health of children and adults.

One of the measurable outcomes of powerlessness in parents may be their tendency to "control." Barsch (1968) demonstrated that mothers of children identified as deficient or different adopt authoritarian attitudes; they become directive and critical, and they tend to interfere with and structure change for their children. Research evidence also indicates that parents of deaf children are more controlling and intrusive than are parents of hearing children (Brinich, 1980; Collins, 1969; Greenberg, 1980; Schlesinger and Meadow, 1972). This phenomenon is interactional, that is, the child evokes powerlessness, which in turn evokes control. Mental health may suffer as a consequence.

DEAFNESS AND MENTAL HEALTH

Although it is said that the deaf population does not have a higher incidence of mental illness per se, researchers indicate that deaf individuals are beset with "more problems of living" (Rainer and Altshuler, 1966; Rainer, Altshuler, and Kallman, 1969). Furthermore, it has been found that deaf school-aged children, when compared with their hearing peers, have five times as much emotional disturbance (Schlesinger and Meadow, 1972). Self-esteem is seen as a crucial component of mental health, and problems of low self-esteem often characterize deaf children and their parents.

Coopersmith (1967) defines four critical variables that influence self-esteem. They include the following: (1) a sense of power, or the ability to shape the environment in mature and age-appropriate ways; (2) significance, or the sense of being valued for being alive; (3) worth, or the ability to live according to the rules of society, and to do so flexibly; and (4) competence, or the ability to perform competently in those areas of life that are important to the individual and to society.

These variables are found more frequently in parents who have high levels of self-esteem and who are able to communicate the rules of society flexibly to their children. In the case of deafness, however, parental self-esteem is often severely traumatized by (1) guilt over bringing forth a child with a deficit, (2) the conflicting advice offered by so-called experts (Schlesinger, 1976). In addition, the parents' ability to explain rules of behavior to their deaf children may be stressed by the absence of shared linguistic symbols and the perplexity and helplessness that result.

The deaf child will be negatively influenced if he or she has a delay in language acquisition and, as a result, continues to influence the environment through physical means when linguistic means are more age-appropriate. Deaf children also frequently receive the parental message, "We'll love you if you become as if hearing," an impossible condition for deaf youngsters to achieve. Furthermore, deaf youngsters receive messages about the rules of society in ambiguous ways. It has been shown that cognitive structuring, which is the most critical variable for appropriate discipline, is not possible without language (Schlesinger, 1978a). Finally, deaf children's sense of competency is frequently impaired since their parents' expectations for competency so often lie in the area most crucially influenced by deafness: speech.

There is nothing inherent in a hearing deficit that should create additional social or psychological problems (Meadow, 1980), yet problems continue as deaf children mature. Deaf preschoolers typically are less competent in many areas that are needed for later achievement and maturity. Compared to hearing children, deaf preschoolers in one study had fewer social interactions but had more physical contact, requests for approval, and negative interactions (Heider and Heider, 1941). Their interactions were also less highly organized and showed less continuity of structure. Without adequate language, they tended to provoke either aggression or withdrawal from their peers in order to gain control of the situation (Heider, 1948). Even in areas in which skills were within the child's repertoire they were not exercised. Deaf preschoolers have been described as immature, impulsive, and less autonomous than their hearing peers (Chess, Korn, and Fernandez, 1971).

This social immaturity seems to increase with age (Burchard and Myklebust, 1942; Myklebust, 1960). One third of deaf youths who leave school each year do not possess the qualifications needed to continue their education or to become employed. The characteristics of such young adults include severely limited communication skills, low levels of academic achievement, emotional immaturity, secondary disabilities, and poor vocational preparation (Rice, 1973).

The most common psychological generalization about deaf adults is that they seem to be emotionally immature. This characteristic has been specified in terms of emotional underdevelopment, a substantial lag in understanding the dynamics of interpersonal relationships and of the world, a highly egocentric life perspective (Levine, 1956), lack of empathy, and impulsivity (Altshuler, 1964). Impulsivity was substantiated in a cross-cultural (American–Yugoslav) study (Altshuler et al., 1976).

DEAFNESS AND LANGUAGE DEVELOPMENT

Young deaf children nearly always experience language deficits or delays. The hearing child at age five is said to know at least 2000 words; a deaf child was said to be unusual if he knew about 200 (Hodgson, 1953). Moreover, without language teaching the deaf five year old child may be expected to know fewer than 25 words (DiCarlo, 1964). When we studied 40 deaf and 20 hearing preschoolers, we found that while the hearing children scored at the expected age level, 75 per cent of the deaf preschoolers, who had a mean age of 44 months, had a language level of 28 months or less (Schlesinger and Meadow, 1972).

Other studies have focused on gesture-language acquisition, spoken language acquisition, and manual language acquisition. When the use of gestures by deaf children of hearing parents was investigated, these gestures were found to be linguistic and to parallel the acquisition of semantic functions in other languages (Goldin-Meadow, 1975). Similarly, most studies examining the spoken language of hearing impaired children who have been taught oral language indicate that the youngsters acquire semantic and syntactic structures in the same sequence, although at a delayed rate, as do hearing youngsters (Juenke, 1971; Hess, 1972). In fact, in a study of the acquisition of bimodal language (a simultaneous combination of signed and spoken English), deaf infants were found to develop sign output earlier than hearing infants developed spoken output. They also had accelerated vocabulary acquisition and semantic growth (Schlesinger, 1978b; Schlesinger and Meadow, 1972).

Many factors crucially affect the early parent-child interaction and communication, and thereby influence language development. These include the onset of deafness, the amount of residual hearing, the audiometric shape of the hearing loss, the absence or presence of other handicaps, and the hearing status of the parents. Certain groups of deaf individuals therefore have a more felicitous outcome. One of these groups is represented by deaf children of deaf parents.

Meadow (1980) summarized a number of studies showing that, compared with deaf children of hearing parents, deaf children of deaf parents have significantly better scores on reading and written language (with no difference on tests of speech and lipreading skills). These youngsters also have a more optimal adjustment in terms of maturity, responsibility, independence, popularity, and adjustment to deafness, and motivation for work. In addition, deaf children with deaf parents have greater impulse control than do deaf children of hearing parents (Harris, 1978). Harris indicates that this may result from the early use of manual communication, which provides the child with a tool for monitoring impulse. We also believe that these differences may exist because most deaf parents welcome their deaf children and are not rendered powerless or helpless by them.

LINGUISTIC STYLES OF CAREGIVERS

There is some evidence that parental linguistic styles at toddlerhood are crucial to the child's development of future competence. In an excellent review chapter on the social bases of language development, Bates, Brertherton, Beeghley-Smith and McNew (1982) indicate that "very little evidence exists for significant correlations between attachment measures and language measures." They further indicate that even other preverbal variables usually postulated to be causal in language acquisition "reveal disappointing results." The low correlation between "good" attachment and language measures is puzzling. Indeed, Kenez (1983) suggests that the attachment literature may not sufficiently "tap" the power-autonomy relationships between mother and infant—relationships that we postulate to be of crucial importance in language acquisition.

Verbal interchanges, however, are clearly causal in language acquisition. One effective variable of verbal interchanges is the extent of language input; more language input from adults is related to more and better language from children. Another variable is the use of "motherese," the language form mothers use to talk with their infants. Only one feature of motherese is not associated with more rapid linguistic development—the use of imperatives (Furrow, 1979). In fact, the extensive use of imperatives may inhibit both language and intellectual development (Bradley and Caldwell, 1976; Newport, Gleitman, and Gleitman, 1977). One study indicates that "the distribution of acts between parent and child is clearly the most important criterion" for the child's future competence (Baldwin, Cole, and Baldwin, 1982).

We are postulating that parents who feel powerless are more likely to interact semantically and syntactically with the intent to "control" rather than to "converse with" their child (McDonald and Pien, 1982; Newport et al., 1977; Snow, 1977b). Parents who communicate with an intent to control use fewer "real" questions, more imperatives, more attention getting devices, more negative actions and verbalizations, more rapid topic changes, and more monologue (talking *at* the child).

Some of the linguistic features noted earlier clearly distinguish the linguistic environment of the advantaged child from that of the disadvantaged child. Specifically, Schacter (1979) found that advantaged mothers talk twice as much to their children, and do so responsively three times as frequently, compared with disadvantaged mothers. Advantaged mothers prohibit activities half as often and give justification for the prohibitions twice as often. Furthermore, Schachter indicates that:

> our educated mothers adjust their communications to the child's affective development, particularly to the early development of the ego. Since the toddler stage is the time of emerging autonomy, the time of psychological birth (Mahler, Pine, and Bergman, 1975), it seems essential to support the child's budding individuality. Our educated mothers tend to provide this support. Failure to do so is likely to produce problems in asserting autonomy with potentially dire consequences for the child's later school performance. The child may not acquire the confidence necessary for sustained goal-directed activity, or may remain enmeshed in a perpetual power struggle with adult caregivers in an attempt to regain his or her psychological birthright . . . . Indeed, ego theory could explain why social class differences in cognitive performance emerge at toddler age, as children begin to assert their power. How can the powerless support the power strivings of their children? (p. 160)

LANGUAGE USE IN TODDLERS AND PRESCHOOLERS

One of the most interesting studies comparing language in advantaged versus disadvantaged toddlers was conducted by Tough (1977). When compared with their advantaged counterparts, the disadvantaged children scored less well on several measures of linguistic structure. They used explicitness or elaboration less frequently; they used pronouns instead of nouns more frequently; and they used adjectives and extensions of verbs to future, conditional, and past tenses less frequently. The disadvantaged children did appear to have these structures within their repertoire, however, and were able to draw on them when pressed or when their own need to be explicit made them essential.

The major difference between children in the advantaged and disadvantaged groups was in the tendency to use language for particular purposes. At the age of three years, the disadvantaged groups were not using language spontaneously for purposes that were already evident in the talk of the advantaged groups. These purposes included recalling and giving detail of past experiences, reasoning about present and past experiences, anticipating future events and predicting the outcome, recognizing and offering solutions to problems, planning and surveying alternatives for possible courses of action, projecting into the experiences and feelings of other people, and using the imagination to build scenes through the use of language for their play (Tough, 1977).

At ages five and seven and a half, these same youngsters continued to differ considerably when presented with pictures to elicit language. The disadvantaged youngsters continued to rely heavily on a labeling strategy, enumerating single objects. In contrast, the advantaged youngsters elaborated more extensively, described a central meaning more frequently, and more often provided causal and dependent relationships, forecasted, and used justification for events.

We are presently reanalyzing some old data to corroborate our hypothesis that mothers of unsuccessful deaf children employ the linguistic codes used by disadvantaged mothers (Schachter, 1979) and that their toddlers are predisposed to use the language strategies found in disadvantaged toddlers (Tough, 1977).

MOTIVATIONAL STANCES IN SCHOOL SETTINGS

Zigler and his colleagues (Zigler and Butterfield, 1968; Zigler and Trickett, 1978) have postulated that affective–motivational factors may be the key elements in disadvantaged children's poor performance both on school tasks and on tests that predict school performance. Such factors have been identified as low self-esteem, "effectance" motivation, and wariness of adults. A long list of maladaptive behaviors in school settings may also be influenced by motivational factors. Lavatelli (1974), for example, indicates that the disadvantaged child has difficulty following directions, participating in discussions, comparing two objects, drawing inferences, and using rules efficiently. The child is further described as demonstrating a communicational egocentrism, as being less active in verbal initiative, as less able to use the teacher as a resource, and as developing severe reading problems, especially around the fourth grade reading level. (It is noteworthy that reading ability at fourth grade level may be related to early reciprocal and responsive language exchanges between mother and child [Loban, 1963; Milner, 1951; Pringle, 1965]). The author of this chapter has heard similar descriptions of deaf children from their teachers.

Deaf children resemble disadvantaged children in their attitudes toward school (Cazden, 1972). Middle class parents socialize their children to go to school to learn, whereas lower class mothers tell their children to be obedient and stay out of trouble (Hess and Shipman, 1965). In our comparison of hearing and deaf children at age eight, 89 per cent of the hearing children said they went to school "to learn," but only 39 per cent of the deaf children gave that response. The remainder went because they "had to."

It would not be surprising—and indeed would be plausible and "adaptive"—that children who were talked "at" rather than "with," who received communicative input replete with imperatives, prohibitions, and constraint questions, would not be entranced with communicative interchanges with adults. Indeed, both disadvantaged and deaf children are said to learn language primarily from their peers. On the other hand, exceptions abound both among the deaf and the disadvantaged populations, and successful outcomes have been seen in both groups.

A longitudinal study we conducted and referred to earlier in this paper has added to these findings (Schlesinger and Meadow, 1972). In that study, 40 deaf youngsters and their mothers were studied over a period of ten years and compared with hearing youngsters and their mothers. As a group the mothers of deaf children were less flexible, permissive, encouraging, and creative; they were more frequently didactic and intrusive. The deaf children were less buoyant, less compliant, and showed less enjoyment of their mothers, and less pride in their achievement. Within this group of deaf children, however, some revealed more successful, meaningful, and gratifying communication with their mothers. These youngsters had a higher level of communicative competence and more closely resembled their hearing peers.

For the first five years of the study, we noted that as the children's communication skills improved, their mothers' behavior increasingly resembled that of the mothers of hearing children, and the deaf children increasingly resembled their hearing peers. In contrast, the deaf children whose communication continued to be poor experienced a growing gap between themselves and their hearing peers; they were seen as enjoying interactions less, as being less independent, creative, or happy, and as exhibiting less pride in their achievements.

These findings, when integrated with the other work described earlier, suggest that when children and parents are able to communicate reciprocally and successfully, they feel more powerful. Their interchanges are marked by a greater sense of mastery and less need for control, and parents are more able to pursue linguistic and psychological stances with their children, which will in turn foster the child's autonomy and enhance his or her motivation to learn.

Researchers working with individuals with other disabilities suggest that similar trends are exhibited by the children and parents in their studies, including blind children (Kekilis, 1981), hyperactive children (Lambert, 1982), and orthopedically handicapped children (Carpignano, 1983).

INTERVENTION STRATEGIES

Intervention strategies may be based on the previously discussed conceptualizations and are presently being researched. Fraiberg (1980) describes how even the most disadvantaged parents can be helped to be responsive to their children. Professionals can sensitively "support and facilitate" the actions of parents, helping them to gain a sense of mastery, competency, and autonomy that will in turn lead to mastery, competency, and autonomy in their youngsters.

REFERENCES

Altshuler, K. Z. (1964). Personality traits and depressive symptoms in the deaf. In J. Wortis (Ed.), *Recent advances in biological psychiatry*, (Vol. 6.) New York: Plenum Press.

Altshuler, K. Z., Deming, W. E., Vollenweider, J., Rainer, J. D., and Tendler, R. (1976). Impulsivity and profound early deafness: A cross cultural inquiry. *American Annals of the Deaf, 131*, 331–345.

Auletta, K. (1982). *The Underclass*. New York: Random House.

Baldwin, A. L., Cole, R. E., and Baldwin, C. P. (Eds.) (1982). Parental pathology, family interaction, and the competence of the child in school. *Monographs of the Society for Research in Child Development, 47*(5), Ser. No. 197.

Barsch, R. H. (1968). *The parent of the handicapped child: The study of child-rearing practices*. Springfield, IL: Charles C Thomas.

Bates, E., Brertherton, I., Beeghley-Smith, M., and McNew, S. (1982). Social bases of language development: A reassessment. In H. Reese and L. Lipsett (Eds.), *Advances in child development and behavior* (Vol. 16). New York: Academic Press.

Boothe, L. L., Lasky, E. Z., and Kricos, P. B. (1981). Comparison of the language abilities of deaf children and young deaf adults. *Journal of Rehabilitation of the Deaf, 15,* 10–16.

Bradley, R. H., and Caldwell, B. M. (1976). The relation of infants' home environments to mental test performance at fifty-four months: A follow-up study. *Child Development, 47,* 1171–1174.

Brinich, P. (1980). Childhood deafness and maternal control. *Journal of Communication Disorders, 13,* 75–81.

Burchard, E. M., and Myklebust, H. R. (1942). A comparison of congenital and adventitious deafness with respect to its effect on intelligence, personality and social maturity. *American Annals of the Deaf, 87,* 140–154.

Carpignano, J. (1983). Personal communication.

Cazden, E. (1972). *Child language and education.* New York: Holt, Rinehart, & Winston.

Chess, S., Korn, S. J., and Fernandez, P. B. (1971). *Psychiatric disorders of children with congenital rubella.* New York: Brunner/Mazel.

Collins, J. L. (1969). *Communication between deaf children of pre-school age and their mothers.* Unpublished Ph.D. dissertation, University of Pittsburgh, PA

Coopersmith, S. (1967). *The antecedents of self-esteem.* San Francisco: W. H. Freeman.

DiCarlo, L. M. (1964). *The deaf.* Englewood Cliffs, NJ: Prentice-Hall.

Durning, P. (1980). Psychose: les parents accusés. Note sur la violence des équipes éducatives ou thérapeutiques à l'égard des parents. *Education et Developpement, 139,* 24–33.

Fraiberg, S. (1980). *Clinical studies in infant mental health: The first year of life.* New York: Basic Books.

Furrow, D. (1979). *The benefits of motherese.* Paper presented at the biennial meeting of the Society for Research in Child Development, San Francisco, March, 1979.

Goldin-Meadow, S. (1975). *The representation of semantic relations in a manual language created by deaf children of hearing parents. A language you can't dismiss out of hand.* Unpublished Ph.D. dissertation, University of Pennsylvania, College Park, PA.

Greenberg, M. (1980). Social interaction between deaf preschoolers and their mothers. *Developmental Psychology, 16,* 465–474.

Greenspan, S. I. (1980). Developmental morbidity in infants in multi-risk-factor families: Clinical perspectives. *Public Health Reports, 16.*

Haggstrom, W. C. (1964). The power of the poor. In F. Riessman, J. Cohen, and A. Pearl (Eds.), *Mental health of the poor.* New York: Free Press.

Harris, R. I. (1978). Impulse control in deaf children: Research and clinical issues. In L. S. Liben (Ed.), *Deaf children: Developmental perspectives.* New York: Academic Press.

Heider, F., and Heider, G. M. (1941). Studies in the psychology of the deaf. *Psychological Monographs, 53,* No. 242.

Heider, G. M. (1948). Adjustment problems of the deaf child. *Nervous Child, 7,* 38–44.

Hess, L. (1972). *The development of transformational structures in a deaf child and a normally hearing child over a period of five months.* Unpublished master's thesis, University of Cincinnati, OH.

Hess, R. D., and Shipman, V. C. (1965). Early experience on the socialization of cognitive modes in children. *Child Development, 34,* 869–886.

Hodgson, K. W. (1953). *The deaf and their problems, a study in special education.* London: C. A. Watts and Company.

Juenke, D. (1971). *An application of a generative-transformational model of linguistic description of hearing impaired subjects in the generation and expansion stages of language development.* Unpublished master's thesis, University of Cincinnati, OH.

Kekilis, L. S. (1981). *Mothers input to blind children.* Unpublished master's thesis, University of Southern California, Los Angeles.

Kenez, P. (1983). Personal communication.

Lambert, N. M. (1982). Temperament profiles of hyperactive children. *American Journal of Orthopsychiatry, 52,* 458–467.

Lavatelli, C. (Ed.) (1974). *Language training in early childhood education.* Urbana, IL: University of Illinois Press.

Levine, E. S. (1956). *Youth in a soundless world, a search for personality.* New York: New York University Press.

Loban, W. (1963). *The language of elementary school children: Research report No. 1.* Champaign, IL: National Council of Teachers of English.

Mahler, M., Pine, F., and Bergman, A. (1975). *The psychological birth of the human infant: Symbiosis and individualism.* New York: Basic Books.

McDonald, L. and Pien, D. (1982). Mother conversational behavior as a function of interactional intent. *Journal of Child Language, 9,* 337–358.

Meadow, K. P. (1969). Parental responses to the medical ambiguities of deafness. *Journal of Health and Social Behavior, 9,* 229–309.

Meadow, K. P. (1980). *Deafness and child development.* University of California Press.

Milner, E. (1951). A study of the relationship between reading readiness in grade one school children and patterns of parent–child interaction. *Child Development, 22,* 95–112.

Minuchin, S., Montalvo, B., Guerney, B. G., Fosman, B. L., and Schumer, F. L. (1967). *Families of the slums: An exploration of their structure and treatment.* New York: Basic Books.

Myklebust, H. (1960). *The psychology of deafness: Sensory deprivation, learning and adjustment.* New York: Grune and Stratton.

Moses, K., and Hecke-Wulatin, M. V. (1978). The socio-emotional impact of infant deafness: A counselling model. In G. T. Mencher and S. E. Gerber (Eds.), *Early management of hearing loss.* New York: Grune and Stratton.

Newport, E., Gleitman, L., and Gleitman, H. (1977). Mother, I'd rather do it myself: Some effects and non-effects of motherese. In C. Ferguson and C. Snow (Eds.), *Talking to children.* London and New York: Cambridge University Press.

Pringle, J. L. K. (1965). *Deprivation and education.* London: Longmans Green.

Rainer, J. D., and Altshuler, K. Z. (1966). *Comprehensive mental health services for the deaf.* New York: New York State Psychiatric Institute, Columbia University.

Rainer, J. D., Altshuler, K. Z., and Kallman, F. J. (Eds.) (1969). *Family and mental health problems in a deaf population.* Springfield, IL: Charles C Thomas.

Rice, B. (1973). *A comprehensive facility program for multiply handicapped deaf adults.* Fayetteville, AR: Rehabilitation Research and Training Center.

Ross, A. E. (1964). *The exceptional child and the family.* New York: Grune and Stratton.

Sadock, B. J., Kaplan, H. I., Freedman, A. M., and Sussman, N. (1975). Psychiatry in the urban setting. In A. M. Freedman, H. I. Kaplan, and B. J. Sadock (Eds.), *Comprehensive textbook of psychiatry II.* Baltimore: Williams & Wilkins.

Schachter, F. F. (1979). *Everyday mother talk to toddlers: Early intervention.* New York: Academic Press.

Schlesinger, H. S. (1976). Emotional support for parents. In D. L. Lillie, P. L. Trohanis, and K. W. Goin (Eds.), *Teaching parents to teach.* New York: Walker and Co.

Schlesinger, H. S. (1978a). The effects of deafness on childhood development: An Eriksonian perspective. In L. S. Liben (Ed.), *Deaf children: Developmental perspectives.* New York: Academic Press.

116   Deafness, Mental Health, and Language

Schlesinger, H. S. (1978b). The acquisition of bimodal language. In I. M. Schlesinger and L. Namir (Eds.), *Sign language of the deaf: Psychological, linguistic, and sociological perspectives*. New York: Academic Press.

Schlesinger, H. S., and Meadow, K. P. (1972). *Sound and sign: Child deafness and mental health*. Berkeley: University of California Press.

Snow, C., Arlman-Rupp, A., Hassing, Y., Jobse, J., Joosten, J., and Uorster, J. (1976). Mother speech in three social classes. *Journal of Psycholinguistic Research, 5,* 1–20.

Snow, C. E. (1977a). The development of conversation between mothers and babies. *Journal of Child Language, 3,* 34–52.

Snow, C. E. (1977b). Mother's speech research: From input to interaction. In C. E. Snow and C. A. Ferguson (Eds.), *Talking to children: Language input and acquisition*. Cambridge: Cambridge University Press.

Tough, J. (1977). *The development of meaning: A study of children's use of language*. New York: Halsted Press.

Zigler, E., and Butterfield, E. C. (1968). Motivational aspects of changes in IQ test performance of culturally deprived nursery school children. *Child Development, 39,* 1–14.

Zigler, E., and Trickett, P. K. (1978). IQ, social competence, and evaluation of early childhood intervention programs. *American Psychologist, 33,* 789–798.

Section IV

TECHNOLOGICAL ADVANCES

Advances in microelectronics and digital circuits have opened up a host of optimistic possibilities for educating young deaf children. However, there is a danger that teachers of the deaf will not be able to incorporate these advances into their daily routines because their training does not prepare them to work with the new generation of assistive devices and teaching aids. Levitt explores the educational opportunities offered with such devices as digital hearing aids and nonauditory aids, as well as the educational and management opportunities offered with electronic record keeping. He also points out the potentially new and powerful teaching strategies offered by computers with speech recognition and production capabilities.

In the second chapter of this section (Chapter 7), Friel-Patti and Roeser describe the results of a longitudinal study of the efficacy of vibrotactile aids for young deaf children learning language. Their approach uses a within-subject design and benefits from a powerful language coding procedure. Their results show a clear increase in both objective language measures and subjective clinical evaluation of vocalizations. Although their results are encouraging, it will be particularly interesting to see the impact of vibrotactile inputs from a device that is truly wearable and whose output frequency range more closely approximates the impedance characteristic of the human skin.

The lessons of these two chapters are occasionally reiterated in workshops at conventions and tutorial vehicles. The full impact of these technological advances will not be realized, however, until more attention to educational technology is paid in the curricula of teachers of the hearing impaired.

Chapter 6

Technology and the Education of the Hearing Impaired

Harry Levitt

Modern technology has had a profound influence on the education of handicapped children, and on hearing impaired children in particular. The hearing aid, auditory trainer, FM speech transmission devices, specialized audiovisual systems, and telecommunication devices for the deaf are all examples of technological aids that have had a direct impact on the education of the hearing impaired.

We are now at the threshold of a new era. The recent development of inexpensive microcomputers and other devices involving digital electronic (e.g., arcade games) has produced a fundamental change in the role of technology on the educational process. There is now a much more positive attitude toward the greater use of technology in the classroom which, in turn, has opened up an abundance of new possibilities. The purpose of this chapter is to examine the ways in which this new technology can be harnessed to improve the education of the hearing impaired.

In discussing technological aids and the hearing impaired, it is important to bear in mind the close link between learning and communication. The effect of a hearing impairment involves more than a reduction in the ability to communicate, especially when the impairment is congenital or acquired very early in life. Such impairments severely impede the development of normal speech and language. Great importance is thus attached to the use of technological aids that will improve communication and that, in turn, will facilitate the development of speech and language in the hearing impaired child.

THE HEARING AID

The most widely used technological aid of all is the conventional hearing aid. Although there is much that can still be done to improve the quality of modern hearing aids, there is little doubt that the introduction of the wearable, personal hearing aid has revolutionized the education of the hearing impaired. Prior to this technological development, schools for the deaf had large numbers of children who essentially were only hard of hearing. Furthermore, these children were condemned to an education designed to prepare them for a subordinate role in society. Times have changed dramatically. The vast majority of children at schools for the deaf today are those who are severely or profoundly hearing impaired, the remainder having been mainstreamed into the regular school system. The educational process is now geared, at least in principle, to provide equal educational opportunity to both normal hearing and hearing impaired children.

These changes came about as a result of several interactive factors: the wide scale introduction of new technology (the hearing aid), the realization of what this new technology could achieve, and concomitant changes in society's attitude towards the hearing impaired.

It is instructive to examine, in this light, what further educational advances may be possible by the application of recent advances in computer technology to facilitate speech communication. One obvious possibility is the digital or computer hearing aid. Experimental digital hearing aids have already been developed (Graupe, 1978; Levitt, 1982b), although a practical, wearable digital hearing aid is not yet available. The experimental devices that have already been developed indicate that digital hearing aids are entirely feasible and that it is only a matter of time before they are generally available.

It is important to recognize that there are both advantages and disadvantages to the use of "computerized" (i.e., digital) hearing aids and that the implementation of this new generation of hearing aids should be geared to maximizing their advantages while circumventing or minimizing their disadvantages. It would be a mistake, for example, to think of the digital hearing aids as simply an improved version of a conventional hearing aid. A digital hearing aid is basically a programmable microprocessor and, as such, can perform functions in addition to simple amplification. Some of the more promising possibilities include the automatic cancellation of acoustic feedback, self-checking and self-calibration, automatic adjustment to different combinations of speech and background noise, and some degree of processing of the speech signal to maximize use of residual hearing. The use of a digital hearing aid also opens the door to more advanced forms of signal processing, such as techniques designed to (1) improve signal-to-noise ratio, (2) reduce the effects of room reverberation, and (3) modify the speech signal itself so as to reduce internal masking effects (e.g., strong components of the speech signal masking much weaker components).

The above-mentioned features are in addition to the hearing aid's basic function as a low cost, acoustic amplification system that can be programmed to best match the needs of each user. The concept of a programmable device is particularly important since it circumvents the usual compromise between mass production and individualized prescription. The same basic circuit or electronic chip can be mass-produced on a large scale and at a low cost per unit, while at the same time individualized prescription is possible because each unit can be programmed for each prospective user at the time the hearing aid is prescribed.

The limitations of digital hearing aids pertain to such practical concerns as size, weight, power consumption, and cost. These practical constraints will be met, in due course, but they are likely to limit the overall flexibility of the first practical digital hearing aids.

Given the potential advantages of the new generation of hearing aids, it is incumbent on educators and researchers to identify which aspects of conventional acoustic amplification systems are most in need of improvement to facilitate the educational process. In a recent large-scale study on speech and language development in hearing impaired children (Levitt, McGarr, and Geffner, submitted for publication), it was found that poor use of hearing aids (such as those characterized by frequent breakdowns, or excessive acoustic feedback, or failure to use available aids) was correlated with poor language development, as was the lack of early intervention.

An important correlate of good speech development (and, to a lesser extent, good language development) was the existence of some high frequency >6 kHz) residual hearing. At schools for the deaf, the proportion of children with high frequency hearing is substantial. In the studies reported by Chasser and Ross (1977) and Levitt and colleagues (submitted for publication), nearly 10 per cent of children at schools for the deaf had some high frequency residual hearing. The proportion with high frequency hearing is believed to be much higher for mainstreamed hearing impaired children. In the study by Gold (1978), for example, nearly half of the children had U-shaped audiograms with hearing levels at 8 kHz better than those at 4 kHz. Despite the importance of high frequency hearing and its prevalence among hearing impaired children, conventional hearing aids do not provide amplification above

5 kHz. This is a serious limitation that should be rectified as soon as possible. A practical problem with high gain, high frequency amplification systems is the greater potential for acoustic feedback. The digital hearing aid, with its capacity for automatic cancellation of acoustic feedback, is a good candidate for this type of amplification.

Other factors known to have an especially deleterious effect on speech perception by the hearing impaired (and by implication, the hearing impaired child's acquisition of speech and language) are background noise and room reverberation. No classroom is entirely free of background noise or unwanted reverberation. Furthermore, it is important to remember that the level of noise or reverberation, or both, that is considered acceptable for normal hearing children may nevertheless interfere substantially with the perception of speech by hearing impaired children in the same classroom.

On the basis of the foregoing observations it would appear that, from an educational viewpoint, the development of the next generation of hearing aids should focus on greater reliability, elimination of acoustic feedback, and reducing the effects of background noise and room reverberation. The current trend toward smaller, less noticeable hearing aids may have cosmetic advantages, but if they do not meet the more important requirements just described they will be of limited benefit to the hearing impaired.

ELECTRONIC COMMUNICATION OF WRITTEN LANGUAGE

Another extremely important technological advance with major ramifications for the education of the hearing impaired involves the electronic communication of written language. Although techniques for transmitting typewritten messages were developed over a century ago (e.g., an early version of the teletypewriter was used on the first railways), these devices were not used by very many people because of their prohibitive cost. The turning point came some 20 years ago when a profoundly deaf physicist invented the acoustic coupler, thereby making it economical to use teletypewriters, or similar devices, over conventional telephone lines (Bellefleur, 1976). Recent advances in the mass production of computer terminals and associated communication equipment have resulted in substantial reductions in the cost of telecommunication devices for the deaf, with concomitant increases in the number of deaf users of such devices.

Another recent development with exciting possibilities is the inexpensive pocket computer. These devices, in addition to their intended application, can also be used for displaying, transmitting, receiving, and storing typed messages (Levitt, 1982a). As such, these devices offer the deaf an opportunity to plug into, at very low cost, the devices that are part of the current revolution in electronic message processing.

The use of electronic mail is growing rapidly, as is use of other forms of computer-based graphical communication. Video games represent a form of interactive graphical communication that provides considerable enjoyment for millions of children, both normal hearing and hearing impaired. The educational impact of these video games, for better or worse, is only beginning to be felt. The power of video games in motivating and maintaining the attention of children of all ages is remarkable, and a special challenge lies in the development of innovative games of this type that will be both enjoyable and instructional for the hearing impaired child.

VISUAL AIDS, TACTILE AIDS, AND COMPUTERS

There is a long history of using electronic video displays in teaching speech to the deaf (Levitt, Pickett, and Houde, 1980). Although experimental evaluations of these devices have typically shown positive results, the use of such devices is not widespread. There is, however, a trend toward greater use of electronic speech training aids at schools for the deaf, as shall be discussed shortly. An important practical limitation of most visual speech-training aids is that they are not wearable. As noted by Boothroyd (1973), a child may do extremely well while being tutored with a desk-mounted speech training aid, but show no carryover to other settings. The possibility of making such displays wearable offers considerable hope for the future.

An experimental wearable visual display is that developed by Upton (1968). In this device, important speech cues (e.g., voicing, frication) are conveyed by means of tiny lights mounted in one lens of a pair of eyeglasses. A modification of this device, the eyeglass speech-reading aid, uses cues reflected from the lens surface, thereby making it easier for the subject to focus on the visual cues (Pickett, Gengel, Quin, and Upton, 1974). A similar device is the autocuer (Cornett, Beadles, and Wilson, 1977) in which symbols similar in concept to those used in cued speech are transmitted by means of special eyeglasses.

The eyeglass speech-reading aid and autocuer were designed primarily as aids to speech reception, but they can also be used to monitor the user's own voice. Experimental evaluations of the eyeglass speech-reading aid show the device to be of benefit in improving speech production (Gengel, 1976). The results of use of the device as a speech-reception aid were not as positive.

A more convenient form of a wearable sensory aid is that in which the cues are transmitted tactually, or electrocutaneously. Although the potential value of supplementary tactile cues in both speech reception and speech reproduction was demonstrated some time ago (Gault, 1926), it was not until recently that practical, wearable tactile aids were developed. Experimental evaluations of these devices on young hearing impaired children are showing positive results with respect to improving both speech production and speech reception (Friel-Patti and Roeser, 1983; Sheehy and Hanson, 1983). More sophisticated, wearable tactile displays are currently being developed in which specific speech cues— for example, voice pitch—are transmitted tactually (Boothroyd, submitted for publication).

An alternative to the use of the sense of touch is the electrocutaneous mode of stimulation. Saunders, Hill, and Simpson (1976) have developed a wearable, electrocutaneous display in which speech spectrum information is transmitted by means of a special belt with electrodes, which is worn around the waist.

Despite a slow start, the use of tactile and visual speech training aids at schools for the deaf is growing. This trend is due in part to the greater availability of such devices, which are now being produced commercially, and in part to the growing body of research data showing positive results with modern speech training aids. A third important development is the rapid growth in the use of personal computers in the classroom. These devices are not only playing a crucial role in upgrading the computer literacy of both students and teachers but are also serving as a catalyst in bringing other aids into the classroom.

EDUCATIONAL MANAGEMENT

The coupling of special-purpose technological aids (e.g., speech training aids) with personal computers has many practical advantages. It is possible, using such systems, to make use of well-established methods of computer assisted instruction as well as to develop highly efficient and convenient methods of record keeping (Osberger, 1982; Nickerson and Stevens, 1973). In one application (McGarr, 1982), a microcomputer-based speech training curriculum allows each child's progress to be tracked efficiently and objectively without burdening the teacher with an onerous record keeping task. As the child completes each stage in the training sequence, the teacher presses a special key on the computer console and an automatic record is made of the stage reached in the training sequence, the child's performance at that level of development, the teaching time required, and other relevant information. From these records detailed learning curves are readily obtained on each child. This information is particularly useful for individualized curriculum planning as well as for identifying problem areas in the curriculum itself.

Perhaps the most important benefit of the modern microcomputer, in addition to the advantages of computer assisted instruction, efficient record keeping, and facilitation of the use of other technological aids, is that it opens the door to future developments. There are many potentially useful applications of the microcomputer in the classroom, but it is important that the microcomputer first be accepted as a basic educational tool.

A VIEW OF THE FUTURE

Two possible future applications of computers that may be of particular value in the education of the hearing impaired include the automatic analysis of language and automatic speech recognition. Both of these problems are extremely complex; and although it is unlikely that a complete solution of either problem will be achieved in the near future, partial solutions of limited applicability have already been found. These limited solutions may be of direct practical value to the hearing impaired.

One example is the use of a computer in analyzing syntactic development in the written language of deaf children (Levitt and Newcomb, 1978; Parkhurst and McEachron, 1980, and submitted for publication). In general, the automatic analysis of English syntax is so difficult that it is questionable whether, in principle, such an analysis can be done reliably without human intervention. This is because the structure of normal English is exceedingly complex, and there is a good deal of overlap between syntax and semantics. It is extremely difficult, for example, to program a machine to analyze and interpret sentences with multiple or hidden meanings.

The written language of deaf children, however, can be analyzed by computer with reasonably good reliability, since fairly simple syntactic forms are commonly used, and the interaction between syntax and semantics is not as subtle as in normal, adult language. In an experimental study that compared human and computer phrase structure analysis of the written language of deaf children, the degree of agreement was in excess of 96 per cent for correctly formed sentences (Parkhurst and McEachron, 1980). The agreement was not as good (roughly 90 per cent) for sentences containing syntactic errors or incomplete forms. On the other hand, human evaluators also differ in their analyses of incomplete and ambiguous sentences.

The automatic analysis of the written or typed language of deaf children opens up new possibilities with far-reaching educational implications. One fairly obvious application is the automatic detailed analysis of large numbers of written language samples to obtain reliable benchmark data on syntactic development in deaf children. One such study has already been completed for both written language samples and tests of syntactic comprehension (Levitt et al., submitted for publication) with several very revealing results. One finding, for example, is that syntactic development in deaf children is not simply delayed or deviant but a combination of both. For children with relatively good language skills, there is some delay with some evidence of deviant forms in more complex structures. For children with poor language skills the data show overwhelmingly large delays with substantial evidence of deviant forms, even at relatively early stages in the developmental sequence.

Information from these tests of syntactic development and comprehension can be extremely useful in educational planning and could not be undertaken without the help of a computer. Given such detailed quantitative benchmarks on language development in the hearing impaired, it is possible, using a variation of these computer programs, to track language development in individual children with much greater precision than has been possible in the past and then to use this information systematically in planning an appropriate curriculum for each child.

A future possible application of computers in the classroom is that of automatic speech recognition. Although the automatic recognition of speech without any constraints on the speaker or vocabulary being used appears to be impossible at present, there are practical solutions to problems of smaller size. Speech-recognition programs are already available commercially for applications in which the vocabulary is severely limited (e.g., no more than 100 words). Such programs could be used in speech training in which the correct production of a specific utterance controls some aspect of a computer game (such as the movement of a spaceship in an arcade type video game). An experimental system of this type has been developed at the Boys Town Institute for Communication Disorders (Watson, Neely and Osberger, 1982).

Another possible application of automatic speech recognition is that of automated or semi-automated captioning. The cost in time and effort of adding captions to films and television is substantial and is a primary factor in limiting the widespread use of this very valuable means of communication for the deaf. If a reliable, automatic system of captioning were available, it could be used not only in the mass media but also in the classroom. An experimental, semi-automatic system of this type is currently being evaluated at the National Technical Institute for the Deaf (Stuckless, 1983). In this system, the teacher's spoken output is first converted to touch-shorthand symbols, then to printed text. A skilled typist proficient in the use of a touch-shorthand typewriter is needed for the first stage. The touch-shorthand symbols are converted to English text automatically by computer. There is three to five second delay between the spoken word and its appearance as English text on the graphic display.

A major practical limitation in the present system is the need for skilled touch-shorthand typists. It is hoped that as the technology of automatic speech recognition improves, the degree of automaticity, and hence the practicality, of such systems will increase.

The preceding discussion provides a brief glimpse of several possible future developments. There are many other possible applications of computers in the classroom, and only a few illustrative examples have been chosen. Given the vast range of possibilities, it is important for educators and researchers to take stock of what is likely to be both educationally beneficial and practical in the near future, and to prepare for the effective use of this new technology.

ACKNOWLEDGMENT

Preparation of this paper and research results reported for the City University of New York were supported by PHS Grant #NS 17764.

REFERENCES

Bellefleur, P. A. (1976). TTY communication, its history and future. *Volta Review, 78,* 107–112.
Boothroyd, A. (1973). Some experiments on the control of voice in the profoundly deaf using a pitch extractor and storage oscilloscope display. *IEEE Transactions on Audio and Electroacoustics, AU–21,* 274–278.

Boothroyd, A. (submitted for publication). IEEE Transactions in Acoustics, Speech and Signal Processing. A wearable tactile intonation display for the deaf.

Chasser, G., and Ross, M. (1977). Ultra-high frequency hearing loss in a deaf school population and its relation to speech intelligibility. Paper presented at the annual convention of the American Speech and Hearing Association.

Cornett, R. O., Beadles, R., and Wilson, B. (1977). Automatic cued speech. Paper presented at Research Conference on Speech Processing Aids for the Deaf. Washington, DC: Gallaudet College.

Friel-Patti, S., and Roeser, R. J. (1983). Evaluating changes in the communication skills of deaf children using vibrotactile stimulation. *Ear and Hearing, 4*, 31–40.

Gault, R. M. (1926). Touch as a substitute for hearing in the interpretation and control of speech. *Archives of Otolaryngology, 3*, 121–135.

Gengel, R. W. (1976). Upton's wearable eyeglass speechreading aid: History and current status. In S. K. Hirsh, D. H. Eldredge, I. J. Hirsh, and R. S. Silverman (Eds.), *Hearing and Davis: Essays honoring Hallowell*, St. Louis: Washington University Press.

Gold, T. G. (1978). *Speech and hearing skills: A comparison between hard-of-hearing and deaf children*. Doctoral dissertation, City University of New York.

Graupe, D. (1978). The development of a hearing aid system with independently adjustable sub-ranges of its spectrum using microprocessor hardware. *Bulletin of Prosthetics, Research, 20*, 10–30.

Levitt, H. (1982a). The use of a pocket computer as an aid for the deaf. *American Annals of the Deaf, 127*, 559–563.

Levitt, H. (1982b). *An array-processor digital hearing aid*. Paper presented at the annual convention of the American Speech and Hearing Association, November, 1982.

Levitt, H., McGarr, N., and Geffner, D. (submitted for publication). *Speech and language development in hearing-impaired children*. ASHA Monographs.

Levitt, H., and Newcomb, W. (1978). Computer-assisted analysis of written language: Assessing the written language of deaf children. *Journal of Communication Disorders, 11*, 257–278.

Levitt, H., Pickett, J. M., and Houde, R. A. (Eds.) (1980). *Sensory Aids for the Hearing Impaired*. New York: IEEE Press.

McGarr, N. (1982). Sensory aids and systematic speech training. Project #1 on PHS Grant #NS 17764-02, Progress Report, October, 1982.

Nickerson, R. S., and Stevens, K. N. (1973). Teaching speech to the deaf: Can a computer help? *IEEE Transactions on Audio and Electroacoustics, AU–21*, 445–455.

Osberger, M. J. (1982). Computer-assisted speech training for the deaf. PHS Grant #NS 16247, Progress Report, March, 1982.

Parkhurst, B. G., and McEachron, M. P. (1980). Computer-assisted analysis of written language: Assessing the written language of deaf children, II. *Journal of Communication Disorders, 13*, 493–504.

Parkhurst, B. G., and McEachron, M. P. (submitted for publication). A computer-based syntactic analysis of the written language of hearing-impaired children. In H. Levitt, N. McGarr, and D. Geffner (Eds.), *Speech and language development in hearing impaired children*. ASHA Monographs.

Pickett, J. M., Gengel, R. W., and Quin, R., and Upton, H. W. (1974). Research with the Upton eyeglass speechreader. Fant (Ed.) *Speech communication*, (Vol. 4). Proceedings of the Speech Communication Seminar, Stockholm, April 1–3. New York: John Wiley and Sons.

Saunders, F. A., Hill, W. A., and Simpson, C. A. (1976). *Speech perception via the tactile mode*. Proceedings of the 1976 IEEE International Conference on Acoustics, Speech, and Signal Processing, pp. 594–597.

Sheehy, P., and Hansen, S. A. (1983). The use of vibrotactile aids with preschool hearing-impaired children. *Volta Review, 85*, 14–26.

Stuckless, R. (1983). Real-time transliteration of speech into print for hearing-impaired students in regular classes. *American Annals of the Deaf, 128*, 619–624.

Upton, H. W. (1968). Wearable eyeglass speechreading aid. *American Annals of the Deaf, 113*, 222–229.

Watson, C. S., Neely, S., and Osberger, M. J. (1983). Personal communication.

Chapter 7

Evaluating Changes in the Communication Skills of Deaf Children Using Vibrotactile Stimulation*

Sandy Friel-Patti and Ross J. Roeser

Formal research on tactile communication aids for the deaf began in the 1920s with Gault's pioneering work (Gault, 1924, 1927a, 1927b). Gault's original "tactile aid" was simply a long hollow tube, and the subject placed his or her hand on one end while the experimenter spoke into the other end, thus providing a single locus of tactile stimulation (Gault, 1924). Results from this work were encouraging; one subject learned to discriminate among 120 different sentences, and another was able to pick up the essence of a story from the tactile patterns alone (Gault. 1924, 1927a).

Since Gault's work, numerous other investigators have built and tested tactile communication devices. In 1973, Kirman (1973) published a thorough review of the literature, and by that time nine more attempts had been made at developing an effective tactile aid for the deaf. Kirman summarized his review by stating that although many of the devices developed have produced encouraging results with isolated words or syllables, and even though some have been very ingenious, no tactile device has shown promise with connected discourse.

Scott (1979) later described the development of a vibrotactile aid, the SRA-10, which was designed specifically for the reception of speech

*Reprinted with permission from Friel-Patti, S., and Roeser, R. J. (1983). Evaluating changes in the communication skills of deaf children using vibrotactile stimulation. *Ear and Hearing, 1*, 31–40.©1983 The Williams & Wilkins Company, Baltimore.

and was evaluated using connected discourse. Whereas most tactile aids had relied on spatial displays for the conveyance of spectral information, the aid developed by Scott uses a temporal approach. That is, rather than relying on change in location of stimulation on the skin as the criterion for perception, the temporal approach uses changes in sensation.

The rationale for the use of temporal display comes from several sources. Empirically, there is the early evidence of Gault (1924, 1927a) that sentence length material can readily be learned and discriminated on the basis of envelope information through a single unit vibrator. The amplitude envelope of speech is a temporal display conveying no spectral information; however, it does convey certain prosodic elements of speech, such as intensity and duration. Cole and Scott (1974) also argue that the waveform envelope provides an acoustic means for the psychological integration of the spectral components of speech. In other words, the spectral structure of speech must be perceptually integrated into a single temporal stream, regardless of how it is broken up spatially by the cochlea. A tactile display of speech should also be presented as a single stream of events.

Empirical data on temporal displays also come from Scott (1979). In his study, subjects performed a same-different discrimination task on syllable length and sentence length material. In one condition subjects felt the recorded stimuli through a bone-conduction vibrator and in another through a five channel, spectral type aid. Subjects fared much better with the spectral aid than with the vibrator at making same-different judgments on the syllable length material. However, performance with the two devices reversed when subjects were given sentences to discriminate. It is argued that the difficulty of using the spectral aid for sentence length units of speech was a function of the perceptual difficulty in ordering five separate channels of information in time.

An additional factor affecting the perception of spatial arrays is pointed out by Geldard (1977). In this investigation of the "reduced rabbit," two vibrators are arrayed on the skin. The first vibrator, at location 1, is activated twice, followed by a single pulse from the second vibrator at location 2. The second pulse, although occurring at location 1, is perceived as occurring somewhere between location 1 and location 2. The precise position at which the second pulse is felt is determined by the temporal relation between it and the third pulse. This finding suggests a problem with spatial displays of speech. That is, the perceived location of stimulation in a spatial array, and hence, the perceived frequency, will be confounded by the temporal relation between events.

The aid developed by Scott was evaluated using a "tracking" procedure first described by DeFilippo and Scott (1978). Although tracking is a term that classically describes a general psychophysical procedure in which the subject is instructed to trace a defined parameter of a specified stimulus, in DeFilippo and Scott's procedure a talker, who reads from a text, presents material to a receiver, who attempts to repeat the text verbatim. Performance is measured by the number of correct words per minute. Scott (1974) reported that the SRA–10 was highly effective in increasing the speech-reading ability of connected discourse using the tracking procedure with three of four normal hearing adult subjects who were functionally deafened.

Based on the significant improvements observed using the SRA-10 vibrotactile aid with adults, a logical extension was to evaluate the efficacy of the instrument with children. In January 1981 we began a series of studies to evaluate the SRA-10 with four profoundly deaf children. Our efforts focused on the use of the aid in the perception and production of isolated speech samples, in the classroom, and in individual therapy sessions. This chapter reports results from our efforts in evaluating the SRA-10 in individual language interaction therapy sessions.

The approach described in this chapter differs significantly from previous attempts to assess tactile aids in children. Previous studies have evaluated the effects of the aid on segmental and suprasegmental aspects of speech perception and production (Engelmann and Rosov, 1975; Goldstein and Stark, 1976; Pickett and Pickett, 1963). Although these studies are critical in understanding the psychophysics of tactile speech inputs, providing data on the nature of perceptual inputs that can be perceived through the tactile mode, they have not given the clinician–educator vital information on the overall efficacy of tactile aids in the therapy or classroom settings. In our studies, we attempted to quantify objective changes in communication, including changes in language, that could be attributed to the use of one type of vibrotactile aid, the SRA-10.

METHODS

Subjects

The four profoundly hearing impaired children (two boys and two girls) were students enrolled in the Callier Center–University of Texas at Dallas preschool program for the deaf. The four children had a mean age at the beginning of the study of 4 years 3 months (range 3;10 to 4;6). The criteria for selecting the subjects included the following: congenital hearing impairment in the severe to profound range; normal intellectual functioning, as measured by the Arthur Adaptation of the

Table 7-1. Identifying Information for the Four Subjects

Subject	Date of Birth	Sex	Age of Identification (months)
1	3/15/77	M	11
2	5/23/77	F	2
3	3/20/77	M	27
4	11/30/77	F	6

Age of Amplification (months)	Pure Tone Average (dB HL) (500, 1000, 2000 Hz)		Speech Awareness Threshold	
	R	L	R	L
15	NR/110	93	90	60
6	98	100	75	70
32	NR/110	NR/110	95	95
12	102	103	70	70

Leiter Scale (a standardized nonverbal measure of intellectual ability); and no known or suspected abnormalities accompanying the hearing impairment. The parents were all normal hearing, there were no other family members who were deaf, and English was the primary language spoken at home. In three children the cause of the deafness was thought to be maternal cytomegalovirus infection, Rh incompatibility, and an undetermined first trimester viral infection. In the fourth the cause was unknown. Each family had participated in a parent–infant intervention program soon after the hearing losses were identified. Additional identifying information for each of the subjects is presented in Table 7-1.

Each of the subjects came from intact middle-class families. The eight parents had a minimum of a high school education; four were college graduates. Although the manual signing skills of the parents varied considerably, each of them had participated in sign language classes and attempted to communicate with their children using total communication.

There is no standardized language test currently available for preschool deaf children using signed English. Therefore, before enrollment in the study in February 1981, the Sequenced Inventory of Communication

Development (SICD) (Hedrick, Prather, and Tobin, 1975) was administered using total communication in an attempt to assess the language ability of the subjects. In addition, it was readministered in May 1982. Even though the SICD does not have normative information for total communication assessment protocols, it was selected because it can be relatively easily adapted to such a procedure, and it includes both receptive and expressive language scales, which yield a detailed profile for communication development. It was necessary to exclude items from both scales because they were not appropriate for either hearing-impaired subjects or for Total Communication administration. There were 11 full items excluded from the receptive scale and 13 full

Table 7-2. Results of SICD Testing for the Four Subjects*

Subject	Receptive Scale			Expressive Scale		
	Test 1	Test 2	Difference	Test 1	Test 2	Difference
1	43	55	+12	28	50	+22
	(63%)	(82%)	(+18%)	(35%)	(63%)	(+26%)
2	36	48	+12	31	51	+20
	(54%)	(72%)	(+18%)	(39%)	(65%)	(+26%)
3	33	49	+16	34	39	+5
	(49%)	(73%)	(+24%)	(43%)	(49%)	(+6%)
4	25	44	+19	22	39	+17
	(37%)	(66%)	(+29%)	(28%)	(49%)	(+21%)
$\overline{X}$	34.2	49.0	+14.7	28.7	44.7	+16.0
	(51.0%)	(73.2%)	(+22.2%)	(36.2%)	(56.5%)	(+19.7%)

*The following items from the SICD were not considered appropriate for hearing impaired children and they were not scored:

Receptive Scale	Expressive Scale
1	4
2	5
3	6
4	8
5	9
7	10
13	11
15	12
24	13
29	15
35	18
	25
	26

items omitted from the expressive scale (see footnote to Table 7–2 for those specific items). Because the children's scores could not be compared to appropriate normative data, it was decided that only the number of items passed should be considered, and scores from the first administration of the test were compared with those from the second administration.

Table 7–2 displays the results of the SICD testing. The total number of items passed and the percentage of items passed of all the items tested are given. All of the children improved from the time of the first test to the second. Improvement would be expected because there were approximately 15 months between the two test dates. From the scores, it is not possible to ascertain the language level of the children compared to normally developing children. However, the finding that scores improved between test 1 and test 2 and that the improvement was comparable across subjects implies that they were progressing in a similar way in their language skills, as would be expected.

Procedures

Intervention Sessions. In addition to enrollment in the preschool program for the deaf, the children were enrolled in a program of language therapy, in which they were seen for 30 minute triweekly, individual therapy sessions. The overall goals for these language interaction sessions were to stimulate communication skills and to maximize potential benefits from the vibrotactile stimulation. The language activities provided the children with opportunities for active participation in the interaction, and they were stimulated to initiate and extend their communicative efforts beyond a specifically requested response. During the course of the study (phases I and II), there were two language clinicians for the four children, and once they were assigned, each child–clinician dyad remained the same.

Evaluation Sessions. Evaluation sessions occurred on a regular basis throughout the study, during which time trained observers monitored the communication behaviors targeted. During these sessions, 15 minute videotape recordings were produced. Allowing a 5 minute warm-up period, 10 minutes of these videotaped sessions provided the record for assessing the communicative changes that occurred throughout the course of the study. The evaluation sessions were performed in a specially designed playroom set up for unobtrusive observation. One wall of the playroom contained an observation window (one-way mirror) through which the videotaping was performed. The video equipment included a videocamera (JVC, model DR-6060U). Time to the nearest second was recorded by an electronic time generator and was superimposed on the lower right portion of the video screen.

Aided Versus Unaided Conditions

In the design of the study, each subject served as his or her own control in that the subjects were evaluated during periods of wearing the vibrotactile aid and comparisons were made to an unaided period. Phase I was an aid-on period and occurred during 16 weeks of the Fall 1981 academic year. During phase I each subject wore the SRA-10 vibrotactile aid an average of 10.5 hours per week (range, 10 to 11 hours) in the classroom setting and in the triweekly individual therapy sessions. Communication behaviors were monitored and analyzed for four sessions of phase I during the initial, middle, and final periods. Sessions 1, 2, and 3 occurred during the Fall academic semester in September, October, and December, respectively, and session 4 was recorded in January, after the usual Christmas break.

Phase II was an aid-off condition and occurred during 14 weeks of the Spring 1982 academic year. Subjects were enrolled in the triweekly individual therapy sessions as well as in daily classroom educational programs, but they did not wear the SRA-10 vibrotactile aid. Communication behaviors were evaluated weekly over an 8 week period during phase II.

During the course of the study, subjects wore their personal hearing aids. In both of the aid-on conditions the vibrotactile aids were checked daily and the teacher used the instruments as often as possible during the classroom activities.

Target Behaviors and Communicative Strategies Monitored

Two separate but related communicative behaviors were evaluated: (1) the communication index which is a measure of socially directed interactions; and (2) language interaction measures, including structural and semantic levels of interaction. The underlying assumption was that the communication index would provide an overall measure of amount of change which resulted from the use of the vibrotactile aid, and the language interaction measures would probe the nature of the changes if they occurred.

Communication Index. It has been demonstrated that normal hearing children express a variety of communicative intentions through nonverbal as well as verbal means (Bruner, 1975; Dore, 1975; Moerk, 1977). These nonverbal behaviors include eye gaze, facial expressions, and hand and arm gestures for pointing, showing, and offering. Nonverbal behaviors are often used by normal hearing children in the very early stages of language development as ways of extending and embellishing their emerging expressive repertoire (Bates, 1976; Carter, 1979). Similarly, the communicative behaviors of young deaf children are predominantly vocalizations produced in conjunction with gestures, whole body actions, facial movements, and gaze behaviors (Carr, 1971). Facility with gestures improves with chronological age, and as deaf children learn a formal manual language system, they combine the formal signs with their own gesture systems (Kretschmer and Kretschmer, 1978).

A communication index was calculated for each evaluation session. The communication index was defined as the total amount of time each child used some form of communication, including vocalization only, sign language only, or combined vocalization and sign language. For each session, a communication index was obtained for both the child and the clinician (teacher). Thus, it was possible to compare the two measures and calculate speaker dominance during the session.

Language Interaction Measures. Language samples, composed of the spontaneous signed utterances produced by the children during the weekly language interaction sessions, were transcribed by a person familiar with the children. The target for each sample was 50 spontaneous, intelligible, nonrepetitive signed utterances; however, most of the samples analyzed contained fewer than 50 utterances. The overwhelming majority of the utterances produced were signed only or signed with accompanying vocalizations, although there was one subject who on three occasions produced a verbal utterance with no accompanying sign. These signed utterances were then scored for both structural and semantic measures. Structural measures included (1) total number of signed utterances produced per session; (2) number of signed multiword utterances; (3) number of signed utterances with verbs explicitly expressed; (4) number of basal sentences in which the noun phrase (NP) and verb phrase (VP) were explicitly expressed; and (5) mean length of signed utterances.

The semantic measures were selected in order to tap the growth and change in both referential and relational meanings expressed by the children (Miller, 1981). For our purposes, referential meaning was explored primarily through analysis of the child's use of individual words. The type-token ration (TTR) indexes lexical diversity, and the procedures suggested by Templin (1957) for computing TTR were followed. Relational meaning was analyzed at the intrasentence level through categorization of the semantic relations expressed. The scheme for semantic categories suggested by Retherford, Schwartz, and Chapman (1981) was used to code the transcripts of the children's signed utterances. Thus the semantic measures included (1) TTR; (2) total number of semantic relations expressed; and (3) total number of different semantic relations in the sample.

Instrumentation

Vibrotactile Aid. The development and basic design of the vibrotactile aid used in this study is described in detail by Scott (1974). Figure 7-1 shows the instrument and how it was worn, and Figure 7-2 is a schematic diagram of the aid. Briefly, the SRA-10 is a battery operated vibrotactile aid to speech-reading. Because the aid is battery powered, it is portable but it is much too large to be wearable. It consists of an input microphone, a processing unit, and three vibrators (Western Electric, model 5A) identical with those found in an electrolarynx (Fig. 7-1A and B). The vibrators are secured in a polyurethane mold and attached to an adjustable elastic belt, which holds them against the skin of the abdomen (Fig. 7-1C).

The design and frequency specifications of the aid are such that there are three spectral channels (Fig. 7-2): (1) a high pass channel at 8000 Hz; (2) a midfrequency channel centered at 2400 Hz; and (3) a low frequency bandpass channel with a low cut off at 250 Hz and a high cutoff at 900 Hz. The high pass channel activates one of the vibrators; the midfrequency channel activates two of the vibrators; and the low frequency channel activates all three vibrators. Operationally, high frequencies activate the center vibrators, midfrequencies activate the two outer vibrators, and low frequencies activate all three vibrators.

Table 7–3 provides ranges of awareness thresholds obtained from three of the hearing impaired subjects in the study and from one normal hearing child ten years of age who was functionally deafened with white noise; the normal hearing subject was included as a control because of the young age of the three hearing impaired subjects. As shown, the use of the aid improved awareness to the moderate to moderately severe range for warbled pure tones between 250 and 8000 Hz, and to the mild to moderate range for speech. Essentially no difference was found between the three young hearing impaired subjects and the normal hearing older child.

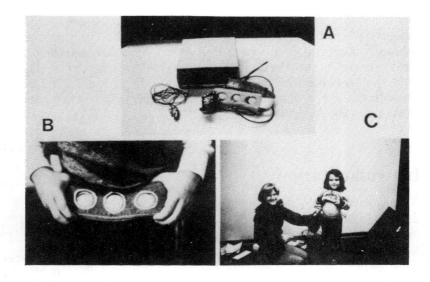

Figure 7-1. The SRA-10 vibrotactile aid consists of a microphone, a processing unit, and three vibrators (*A* and *B*). The vibrators are housed in a polyurethane mold (*B*) and are attached to an elastic belt that holds them against the skin of the abdomen (*C*).

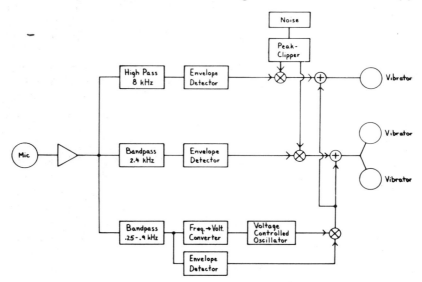

Figure 7-2. Schematic diagram of the SRA–10. From Scott, B. L. (1974). Speech perception: Theory and application. Unpublished doctoral dissertation, University of Waterloo, Ontario. Used with permission.

Table 7–3. Range of Awareness Thresholds for Speech and Warbled Pure Tones Using the SRA–10 (dB HL)

Speech Awareness	250	500	750	1000	1500	2000	3000	4000	6000	8000
30–40	40–55	40–60	50–55	50–55	55–65	50–65	50–65	60–65	60–75	60–80 55–60

Computer Based Observation System. The communication index was obtained using a custom designed, computer based observation system. Because of the nature of the behaviors observed, a continuous, real time measurement, or event sampling strategy, was used. Continuous event sampling involves measurement of the onset and duration (elapsed time between onset and offset) of each instance of the target behaviors during an observation session. The behavioral observations were made using an event recorder system (S & K Products), which worked in conjunction with a microcomputer (Apple II Plus) equipped with a Mountain Hardware Appleclock. The occurrence of an event was recorded by a trained observer who depressed a key on the keyboard. Each time a key was depressed and released, the computer recorded the time at which it was depressed and the time it was released. The basic unit of time used was one second. At the end of each observation session, the data were stored on a minidisk, and a complete listing of the data, which preserved the order of occurrence of each of the behaviors collectively, was printed. Such a data record permitted sequential analyses of time-related patterns and cycles in the flow of behaviors.

A team of four observers was trained on all four behaviors until a minimum criterion of 90 per cent interobserver agreement was achieved. Agreement was calculated on a point-by-point comparison for a full 10 minute session using the standard computational formula of agree/agree = disagree × 1000 = per cent agreement (Sackett, 1978). In all cases, criterion agreement was reached in less than five hours of training. Training of observers was accomplished using videotape recordings, and it was only after criterion had been attained that the observers followed a weekly rotation schedule so that each of the observers was rotated systematically across the four target behaviors. Interobserver agreement was checked on an intermittent and unannounced basis, as suggested by Sackett (1978) as the best method available for maintaining high levels of agreement.

Figure 7–3 shows an example of the data provided by the computer-based observation system. In this example, the top of the figure shows

Response Name	No. of Responses	Total Duration (sec)	Mean Duration (sec)	Standard Deviation (sec)
CVOC	34	223	6.6	5.3
CSIGN	35	178	5.1	4.2
CDRES	22	151	6.9	5.3
CSRES	12	37	3.1	1.0
TRESP	43	281	6.5	4.9
TVOC	41	373	9.1	8.7
TSIGN	40	339	8.5	7.2

Figure 7–3. Example of data provided from the computer-based observation system. The top is a second-by-second record of the observed responses for 10 minutes (600 s). CVOC = child vocalization, CSIGN = child sign, TVOC = teacher vocalization, and TSIGN = teacher sign. CDRES, CSRES, and TRESP are codes for response behaviors recorded in another part of the study not described in this chapter. The bottom is the summary of second-by-second record, which provides the number of responses observed, total duration, mean duration, and standard deviation.

a second-by-second record of the responses being monitored for a ten minute period (600 s). For example, CVOC is child vocalization, CSIGN is child signing, TVOC is teacher vocalization, and TSIGN is teacher signing. The asterisks in the top chart indicate that the response being monitored was occurring at the second-by-second analysis, and the bottom chart shows the number of responses, total duration, mean duration, and standard deviation for each of the responses. This type of summary was available for each evaluation session in phases I and II.

RESULTS

Communication Index

The mean group data for the communication index are displayed in Figure 7–4. Recall that the communication index was operationally defined as the total amount of time each child used some form of communication, including vocalization only, sign language only, or a combination of vocalization and sign language. Inspection of Figure 7–4 shows a sharp rise in the performance of the subjects during phase I. This was followed by a gradual decrease in performance across the eight sessions of phase II.

The improvement seen in phase I could have been related to the use of the vibrotactile aid, the result of the intervention program, or perhaps a combination of these two factors. However, the decrease in performance seen in phase II would strongly indicate that the aid provided benefit for the subjects, as all conditions remained essentially the same with the exception that the aid was removed from the language intervention sessions.

To analyze further the nature of the changes that occurred between aid-on (phase I) and aid-off (phase II), the responses making up the communication index were analyzed separately; Table 7–4 shows these data. During phase I (aid-on), vocalization only and sign only appeared to show little change over the four evaluation sessions. However, the use of vocalization plus sign increased noticeably during this phase, going from 48 s for evaluation session 1 to 183.7 s for session 4. During phase II (aid-off) more variability was present. Vocalization only did not appear to change. However, sign only showed a gradual increase and vocalization plus sign decreased sharply.

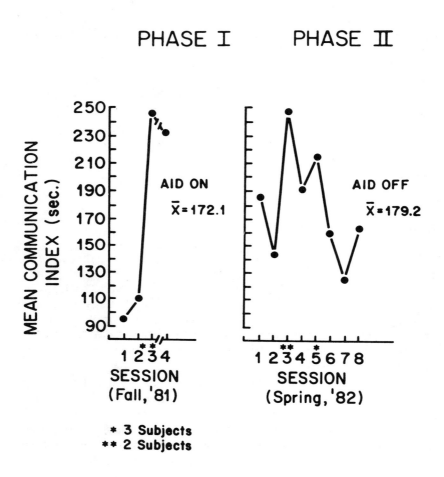

Figure 7–4. Mean communication index for phases I and II. The communication index is the amount of time each child used some form of communication during the language session, including vocalization only, sign language only, or vocalization and sign language.

Regression analyses (Winer, 1971) on each of the three responses for the two phases showed that the slope differences between phases I and II were not significantly different at the 0.05 level of confidence for vocalization only ($t = -0.25$; $df = 39$) or sign only ($t = 2.07$; $df = 39$) measures. However, the difference between phases I and II was

Table 7–4. Mean Number of Seconds in Which Subjects Responded by Vocalizing Only, and by Vocalizing and Signing

	Phase I (Aid-On) Evaluation Session			
	1	2*	3*	4*
Vocalization only	31.0	38.3	8.0	34.5
Sign only	17.0	16.6	32.0	14.5
Vocalization plus sign‡	48.3	57.0	207.3	183.7

	Phase II (Aid-Off) Evaluation Session							
	1	2	3†	4	5	6	7	8
Vocalization only	38.0	20.5	62.0	32.5	57.3	22.0	37.2	50.0
Sign only	18.8	20.0	37.5	22.5	42.0	31.0	28.0	45.5
Vocalization plus sign‡	133.0	102.0	149.5	137.0	117.3	106.0	55.8	73.8

*Three subjects only.
†Two subjects only.
‡Change from phase I to phase II was significant at 0.01 level of confidence (t = 4.56; df = 39).

significant beyond the 0.01 level of confidence for the vocalization plus sign (t = 4.56; df = 39) measure. Overall, these data indicate that the effect of using the aid was to improve the child's use of communication involving sign language plus vocalization (total communication).

Structural Language Measures

Figure 7–5 displays the results of the five structural language measures for the two phases of the study. Inspection of the figure reveals that there was a general trend for the children's performance to rise during phase I and to generally level off or decrease slightly during phase II. The mean number of signed utterances produced by the children essentially remained the same from phase I ($\overline{X}$ = 31.8; range = 23.3 to 39.0) to phase II ($\overline{X}$ = 31.3; range = 24.5 to 34.5). Unsurprisingly, there was a similar pattern with the number of signed multiword utterances produced by the four subjects: the mean for phase I was 14.6 (range = 1.5 to 26.5) compared with the mean for phase II of 16.6 (range = 9.5 to 24.0). The number of explicit verbs produced by the children showed a similar pattern, with the means for phases I and II being 14.1 (range = 2.6 to 22.8) and 17.1 (range = 10.0 to 26.0), respectively. The measure of basal sentences, on the other hand, peaked in phase I with a mean 11.5 sentences (range = 0.50 to 21.8) and dropped dramatically in phase II to 4.3 (range = 0.50 to 6.0). The only measure that appeared to remain somewhat constant was the mean length of the signed utterances for the children. The means for phases I and II were 1.68 (range = 1.10 to 2.09) and 1.74 (range = 1.35 to 2.00), respectively.

The fact that the mean length of signed utterances did not appear to change much while the number of basal sentences declined is somewhat puzzling. Essentially, even though the children were producing longer signed utterances, they were not expressing themselves in NP and VP constructions. Such grammatical constructions are basic to the common grammatical order of spoken English. Because signed English also follows the grammatical ordering of spoken English, it was expected that the children would demonstrate an increase in the number of basal sentences over the time span of the study. That this was not the case could possibly be related to the nature of the conversational exchanges that occurred between the children and their clinicians. That is, it is possible that the language used to accompany the interaction activities was simply object or action oriented and thus resulted in frequent use of nouns, adjectives, and verbs. Furthermore, the nature of a manual–gestural communication system is such that efficiency and ease of communication frequently result in deletion of redundant information. In such cases, the language may indeed be quite rich, but it would not necessarily be scored as a basal sentence because either the NP or the VP may not have been explicitly expressed.

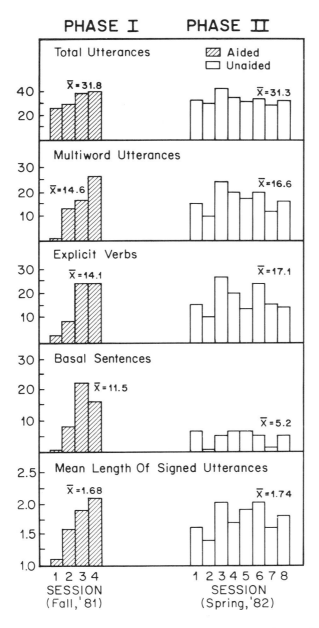

Figure 7-5. Mean structural measures for the language interaction session for phases I and II. See text for explanation.

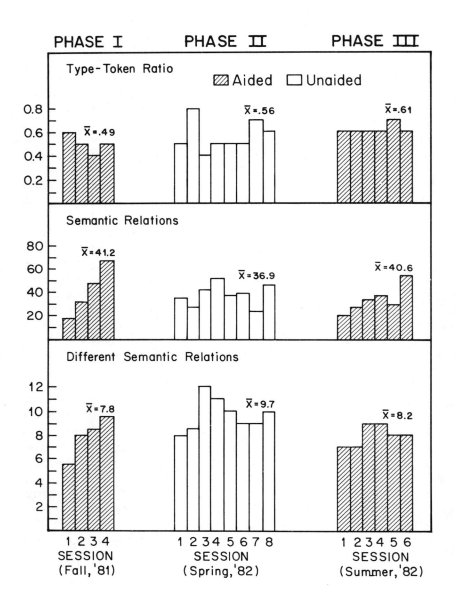

Figure 7–6. Mean semantic measures for the language interaction sessions for phases I, II, and III. See text for explanation.

Semantic Language Measures

Figure 7–6 displays the data for the semantic language measures for the three phases of the study. In general, the pattern seen with the structural language measures did not hold for the semantic measures. That is, in the case of the semantic measures, there was a general tendency to see little difference in the measures from phase I to phase II. The TTR is a measure of vocabulary diversity for the language samples collected. Essentially, for normal hearing children under the age of eight years, it is expected that the TTR will center between 0.40 and 0.60 if the sample is sufficiently large. Templin (1957) reported TTRs of 0.50 for the 480 children she sampled, and this ratio was consistent across age, sex, and socioeconomic status. It is this consistency of the measure which makes it valuable as a clinical tool.

TTRs greater than 0.60 indicate that the sample is small and likely not fully representative of the child's production system, whereas TTRs less than 0.40 indicate that there was a great deal of repetition and redundancy in the sample. Such sparse vocabulary is often considered indicative of a language learning deficiency for normal hearing children. The measure of TTR can thus be used as a check on the adequacy of the sample in terms of vocabulary diversity. For the two phases of the study reported, the TTR stayed within the normal limits established for normal hearing subjects. Thus, for referential meaning, the subjects' performance showed good lexical diversity.

The number of semantic relations expressed by the children in the samples showed a slight decline from phase I ($\overline{X}$ = 41.2; range = 18.25 to 48.5) to phase II ($\overline{X}$ = 36.9; range = 23.3 to 50.5). However, the number of different semantic relations used by the children showed very little variation from phase I ($\overline{X}$ = 7.8; range = 5.5 to 9.5) to phase II ($\overline{X}$ = 9.7; range = 7.6 to 12.0). The number of semantic relations and the number of different semantic relations were measures selected to tap the relational meanings expressed by the children at the intrasentence level. It is not particularly surprising that these measures did not show much change because they are related to the deep structure of the utterance produced, and as such they would be expected to demonstrate only gradual change over the course of the study.

Discussion

Over nine months, we evaluated the efficacy of a particular vibrotactile aid, the SRA-10, with four profoundly deaf children. The overall goal of our project was to assess the benefits from the aid on the perception and production of isolated speech sounds, as an aid to communication in the classroom, and in individual language therapy sessions. This chapter reports the results of our efforts in individual language interaction therapy sessions. In phase I the children wore the vibrotactile aid. The aid was removed during phase II, but all other aspects of the program remained the same.

The four subjects were selected so that factors which were likely to affect their performance in the study were carefully controlled. Thus hearing losses, family backgrounds, and early educational histories were similar. The four children displayed a wide range of communicative skills as measured by the SICD results from February 1981; however, they all followed similar progression patterns between the first and second administrations of the test.

The measures used in this study were obtained during a period of interaction between child and clinician, and every effort was made to keep these interaction sessions as consistent, natural, and representative as possible. Our measurements were also objective in nature and certainly proved to be highly reliable for inter-rater agreement.

The overall pattern of performance measured by the communication index included an initial burst of improvement in phase I. Although this initial improvement was encouraging, it was not possible to separate clearly the effect of the aid from that of the training, as both occurred simultaneously. In an attempt to make such a differentiation, the aid was taken off the children during phase II and the training remained the same. The data from phase II showed noticeable decline in the measure of vocalization plus sign and thus confirmed the suggestion that the improvement resulted from the effect of the aid rather than from the training. The fact that vocalization plus sign increased with the aid on and decreased when the aid was removed is encouraging. For our subjects, vibrotactile stimulation appears to be positively associated with a total communication act. While using the SRA-10, the children seemed to independently establish the association of vocalization plus sign for purposeful communication.

Subjective observations should also be pointed out. There were no adverse reactions by the children toward using the vibrotactile aid, and on several occasions the children voluntarily requested that they be allowed to wear the instruments. Also, teachers, clinicians, and parents reported spontaneously on several occasions that eliciting vocalization was much easier while the children were wearing the aids.

The language interaction measures were obtained in order to probe the nature of the changes that were seen in the communication index, and results essentially paralleled the findings from the communication index. The language interaction measure that decreased markedly when the aid was removed was the measure for basal sentences, indicating that the children were not encoding as much structural information in their communicative efforts. As with the change seen in the mean length of signed utterances in phase II, this finding appears to be more closely linked with the nature of the conversational interaction occurring between the clinicians and the children than with the use of the vibrotactile aid.

Those interested in language development in deaf children may have noted that there was more variability with the structural language measures than with the semantic measures across the two phases of the study. Although interesting, this is not necessarily surprising because the structural measures are linked to the surface form of the message while the semantic measures are directly related to the underlying meaning. Thus, while there was some change in the semantic measures during the project, the change was gradual. This finding is in line with what is known to occur in the language development of normal hearing children. The surface forms, on the other hand, are more difficult to interpret because we are describing structural factors of children using a predominantly manual–visual–spatial communication system.

Our study differs from previous attempts to assess tactile stimuli in children in that we have monitored changes in communication skills of our subjects during periods of connected discourse and manual and gestural communicative attempts along with vocal efforts. Others have assessed changes in perception and production of isolated, minimally different speech samples. Most past studies have shown encouraging benefits from the use of the various tactile aids investigated in the discrimination of isolated speech sounds after an extensive number of training sessions (Engelmann and Rosov, 1975; Goldstein and Stark, 1976; Pickett, 1963; Pickett and Pickett, 1963). As part of our project, we have found evidence that the SRA-10 is also effective in improving the perception and production skills of our subjects when isolated speech samples are used (Bond and Scott, 1982). From the data reported in this chapter, we conclude that the SRA-10 is also helpful in improving the amount of communication in connected discourse in profoundly deaf children when sign plus vocalization is used. Comparable studies are needed using different tactile aids before further conclusions can be drawn regarding other types of stimulation or arrays.

During the two aid-on conditions, which totaled 22 weeks, subjects wore the aid an average of 9 hours per week. Considering the effort made in placement and monitoring the use of the aid, the amount of time the aid was worn appears low. However, it should be remembered that in its present configuration the aid is portable, but it is much too large to be worn on the body, and this factor severely limited additional wearing time. We strongly believe that only body-worn instruments should be used in future studies assessing the long-term benefits from any tactile aid, so that the aid can be worn unobtrusively during the course of the day. In fact, an interesting question is to what extent would the results from this study have differed had it been possible for the subjects to wear the aid for four to six hours per day throughout their educational program.

A final point is that the observation system we developed can be adapted for evaluating different types of communicative devices—for example, other types of tactile aids, monaural versus binaural amplification, or perhaps cochlear implants. There are three advantages of the computer-based observation system that permit this flexibility. The first is that the measurements constituting the communication index were made objectively by a team of observers. The observers in this study were trained in less than five hours, and interobserver agreement remained at or above 90 per cent for all behaviors. The second is that the microcomputer and event recorder used are both portable and can be taken to a variety of observation settings and therefore are not limited to the videotape laboratory. The third advantage is the relatively low cost of the equipment.

ACKNOWLEDGMENTS

We wish to acknowledge the contributions of the other members of the research team, including Brian L. Scott, Terri Siegel Henderson, Sandi L. Bond, Glynn Rasor, Lloyd Smith, and Wende Yellin. We also wish to thank the families of our subjects for their participation in our project.

The research reported in this chapter was supported by National Institutes of Health Grant 1R01 NS 15982-01A1.

REFERENCES

Bates, E. (1976). *Language and context: Studies in the acquisition of pragmatics.* New York: Academic Press.

Bond, S. L., and Scott, B. L. (1982). Evaluating a tactile aid on four-year-old profoundly deaf children. Paper presented at the 103rd Meeting of the Acoustical Society of America, Chicago.

Bruner, J. (1975). The otogenesis of speech acts. *Journal of Child Language, 2,* 1–19.

Carr, M. (1971). Communicative behavior of three and four year old deaf children. Unpublished doctoral dissertation, Teachers College, Columbia University, New York.

Carter, A. (1979). Prespeech meaning relations: An outline of one infant's sensorimotor morpheme development. In P. Fletcher and M. Garman (Eds.), *Language acquisition.* Cambridge: Cambridge University Press.

Cole, R., and Scott, B. L. (1974). Toward a theory of speech perception. *Psychology Review, 81,* 348–474.

DeFilippo, C. L., and Scott, B. L. (1978). A method for training and evaluating the reception of ongoing speech. *Journal of the Acoustical Society of America, 63,* 1186–1192.

Dore, J. (1975). Holophrases, speech acts and language universals. *Journal of Child Language, 2,* 21–40.

Engelmann, S., and Rosov, R. (1975). Tactual hearing experiment with deaf and hearing subjects. *Journal of Exceptional Children, 41,* 243–253.

Gault, R. H. (1924). Progress in experiments on tactual interpretation of oral speech. *Journal of Abnormal Social Psychology, 14,* 155–159.

Gault, R. H. (1927a). Interpretation of spoken language when the feel of speech supplements vision of the speaking face. *Volta Review, 30,* 379–386.

Gault, R. H. (1927b). Hearing through the sense organs of touch and vibration. *Franklin Institute Journal, 204,* 329–358.

Geldard, F. A. (1977). Cutaneous stimuli, vibratory, and saltatory. *Journal of Investigative Dermatology, 69,* 83–87.

Goldstein, M. H., and Stark, R. E. (1976). Modification of vocalizations of preschool deaf children by vibrotactile and visual displays. *Journal of the Acoustical Society of America, 59,* 1477–1481.

Hedrick, D., Prather, E., and Tobin, M. (1975). *Sequenced inventory of communication development.* Seattle: University of Washington Press.

Kirman, J. H. (1973). Tactile communication of speech: a review and an analysis. *Psychology Bulletin, 80,* 54–74.

Kretschmer, R., and Kretschmer, L. (1978). *Language development and intervention with the hearing impaired.* Baltimore: University Park Press.

Miller, J. (1981). *Assessing language production in children.* Baltimore: University Park Press.

Moerk, E. (1977). *Pragmatic and semantic aspects of early language development.* Baltimore: University Park Press.

Pickett, J. M. (1963). Tactual communication of speech sounds to the deaf: Comparison with lipreading. *Journal of Speech and Hearing Disorders, 28,* 315–330.

Pickett, J. M., and Pickett, B. H. (1963). Communication of speech sounds by a tactual vocoder. *Journal of Speech and Hearing Research, 6,* 207–221.

Retherford, K., Schwartz, B., and Chapman, R. (1981). Semantic roles in mother and child speech: Who tunes in to whom? *Journal of Child Language, 8,* 583–608.

Sackett, G. (1978). Measurement in observational research. In G. Sackett (Ed.), *Observing behavior (Vol. II: Data Collection and Analysis Methods).* Baltimore: University Park Press.

Scott, B. L. (1974). Speech perception: Theory and application. Unpublished doctoral dissertation, University of Waterloo, Waterloo, Ontario.

Scott, B. L. (1979). Development of a tactile aid for the profoundly hearing impaired: Implications for use with the elderly. In M. Henoch (Ed.), *Aural rehabilitation for the elderly*. New York: Grune and Stratton.

Templin, M. (1957). *Certain language skills in children: Their development and interrelationships*. Child Welfare Monograph No. 26. Minneapolis: University of Minnesota Press.

Winer, B. (1971). *Statistical principles in experimental design* (Ed. 2). New York: McGraw-Hill Book Company.

AUTHOR INDEX

A

Aksu, A.A., 36, 47
Altshuler, K.Z., 103, 106, 108
Aranow, M.S., 78, 80
Ashbrook, E., 36
Auletta, K., 103, 105

B

Baker, C., 24
Baker, D., 79, 80
Baldwin, A.L., 110
Baldwin, C.P., 110
Barsch, R.H., 107
Bates, E., 109, 138
Beadles, R., 123
Beeghley-Smith, M., 109
Bellefleur, P.A., 122
Bellugi, U., 24, 25, 35, 38, 39, 40, 42, 48, 54
Bergman, A., 110
Berman, R., 28, 47
Bond, S.L., 151
Boothe, L.L., 104
Boothroyd, A., 123, 124
Bradley, R.H., 109
Brertherton, I., 109
Brinich, P., 106
Brown, R., 38
Bruner, J., 138
Burchard, E.M., 107
Buscaglia, L., 86
Butterfield, E.C., 111

C

Caldwell, B.M., 109
Calvert, D.R., 68, 69
Carpignano, J., 113
Carr, M., 138
Carter, A., 138
Casterline, D., 39
Cazden, E., 112
Chapman, R., 139
Charney, R., 29
Chasser, G., 121

Chess, S., 107
Chiat, S., 29
Clark, E.V., 29
Cokely, D., 24
Cole, R., 132
Cole, R.E., 110
Collins, J.L., 106
Contract Research Corporation, 4
Coopersmith, S., 106
Corbett, E., 17
Cornett, R.D., 123
Croneberg, C.G., 39

D

DeFilippo, C.L., 132
Deming, W.E., 103, 108
Deutsch, W., 29
DiCarlo, L.M., 108
Dore, J., 138
Dunn, L.M., 72
Durning, P., 106

E

Eccarius, M., 76
Engelmann, S., 133, 151

F

Fernandez, P.B., 107
Fischer, S., 35, 36
Fosman, B.L., 105
Fraiberg, S., 113
Freedman, A.M., 103
Friedlander, B.Z., 85
Friel-Patti, S., 124
Furrow, D., 109

G

Gallagher, J.J., 4, 5
Garner, W.R., 6

SUBJECT INDEX

Page numbers in *italics* refer to illustrations; (t) indicates tables

A

ASL. *See* American Sign Language.
Acquisition of knowledge, from research into hearing impairment, 6-10, 7(t)
American School Achievement Test, 77-78
American Sign Language, 14-15, 21, 23-56
  distinction between nouns and verbs in, 39-48, *41*, *46*
  morphological systems in, 23-28, *26*, *27*
  spatial marking for verb agreement in, 34-39, *37*
  spatially organized syntax in, 48-51, *50*
  three-dimensional morphology of, 25-28, *26*, *27*
  transition from gesture to sign in, 28-34, *31*
Anger, as state of parental grieving, 94-97
Anxiety, as state of parental grieving, 97-98
Application of knowledge, from research into hearing impairment, 6-10, 7(t)
Auditory Association Subtest of ITPA, 72-73, *73*

C

Classroom communication, and educational programs for hearing impaired children, 16-17
Communication index, in vibrotactile stimulation research, 138, 143-145, *144*, 145(t)

Communication skills of hearing impaired children. *See* Hearing impaired children, communication skills of.
Computer based observation system, used in vibrotactile stimulation research, 141-143, *142*
Computers, as educational aids for hearing impaired children, 123-124
Coping with grief, in parents of hearing impaired children, 100-102

D

DSS, 76-77
Deaf children. *See* Hearing impaired children.
Deafness and language development, 103-116
Deafness and mental health, 103-116
Deficits in hearing, as factor in mental health of hearing impaired children, 103-106
Demonstration projects, defined, 4
Denial, as state of parental grieving, 87-90
Depression, as state of parental grieving, 92-94
Developmental Sentence Scoring System, 76-77

E

Education, programs for hearing impaired children, 3-20
classroom communication in, 16-17
goals of, 16
holistic approach used in, 85
influence of technology in, 119-129
interpreters used in, 17-18
issues in, 13-19
options in, 13-19
prior to rubella epidemic, 11-12
problems of, 12
secondary, 18-19
social influences on, 10-11
technology as influence on, 119-129
testing and, 57-81
Educational management, and technological advances in education of hearing impaired children, 124-125
Electronic communication of written language, as educational aid for hearing impaired children, 122-123
Emotional considerations in birth of hearing impaired children, 83-102
grief of parents and, 85-102
anger as a state in, 94-97
anxiety as a state in, 97-98
coping with, 100-102
denial as a state in, 87-90
depression as a state in, 92-94
grief counseling for, 99-100
guilt as a state in, 90-92
EPIC Test, 67-72, 79-80,*70*, 71(t), *80*
Experimental Program in Instructional Concentration (EPIC), 67-72, 79-80, *70*, 71(t), *80*

G

GAEL-S Test, 58-70, 61(t), *62,64,65,66,70*
GAWL Test, 76-78, *78*
Grammatical Analysis of Elicited Language, 58-70, 61(t), *62, 64, 65, 66, 70*
Grammatical Analysis of Written Language, 76-78, *78*
Grammatical Closure subtest of ITPA test, 74, *74*

Grief counseling, for parents of hearing impaired children, 99-100
Grieving, as response to infant deafness. *See* Emotional considerations in birth of hearing impaired children.
Guilt, as state of parental grieving, 90-92

H

Hearing aids, 120-122
Hearing impaired children,
assessment of academic performance of, through testing, 57-81
birth of, emotional considerations in. *See* Emotional considerations in birth of hearing impaired children.
communication skills of, evaluation of using vibrotacile stimulation, 131-154, (*See also* Vibrotactile stimulation)
communication with parents, 14-15
conditions relating to variation in academic achievement of 12-13
development of language in, 103-116
programs for, 18-19 (*See also* Education, programs for hearing impaired at secondary level)
classroom communication and, 16-17
holistic approach used in, 85
goals of, 16
interpreters used in, 17-18
technological advances in, 119-129
testing and, 57-81
influence of linguistic styles of care-givers on, 109-110
mental health of, 103-116
powerlessness as a factor in, 103-106
performance in school, 111-113
Hearing impairment, research on, 3-9 (*See also* Research on hearing impairment)
Holistic approach to habilitation of hearing impaired children, 85

I

ITPA, 72-74, *73, 74*
Illinois Test of Psycholinguistic Abilities, 72-74, *73, 74*